ZiGGY'S®

SCHOOL OF HARD KNOCKS

Other Ziggy Books

Ziggy's Follies
Ziggy in the Fast Lane
Ziggy's Ups and Downs
Ziggy's Place
Alphabet Soup Isn't Supposed to Make Sense
Ziggy's Big Little Book

ZIGGY'S®
SCHOOL OF HARD KNOCKS

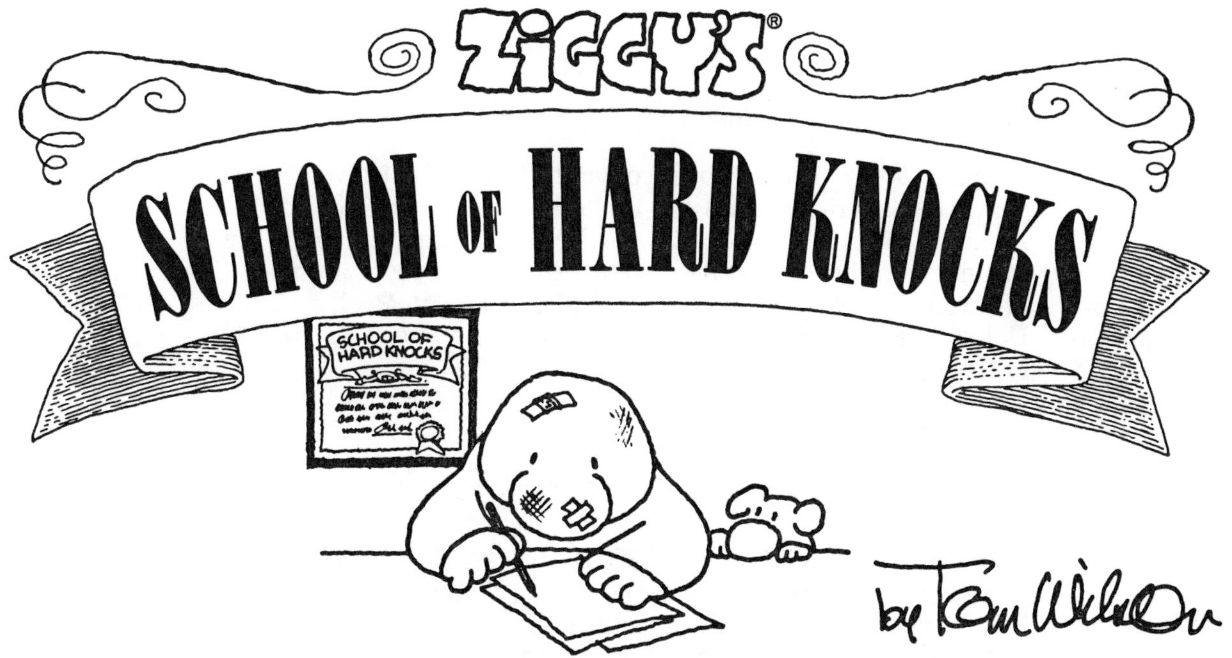
SCHOOL OF HARD KNOCKS

by Tom Wilson

Andrews and McMeel
A Universal Press Syndicate Company
Kansas City • New York

Ziggy ® is syndicated internationally by Universal Press Syndicate.

ISBN: 0-8362-1839-6

Library of Congress Catalog Number: 88-83870

ATTENTION: SCHOOLS AND BUSINESSES

Andrews and McMeel books are available at quantity discounts with bulk purchase for educational, business, or sales promotional use. For information, please write to: Special Sales Department, Andrews and McMeel, 4900 Main Street, Kansas City, Missouri 64112.

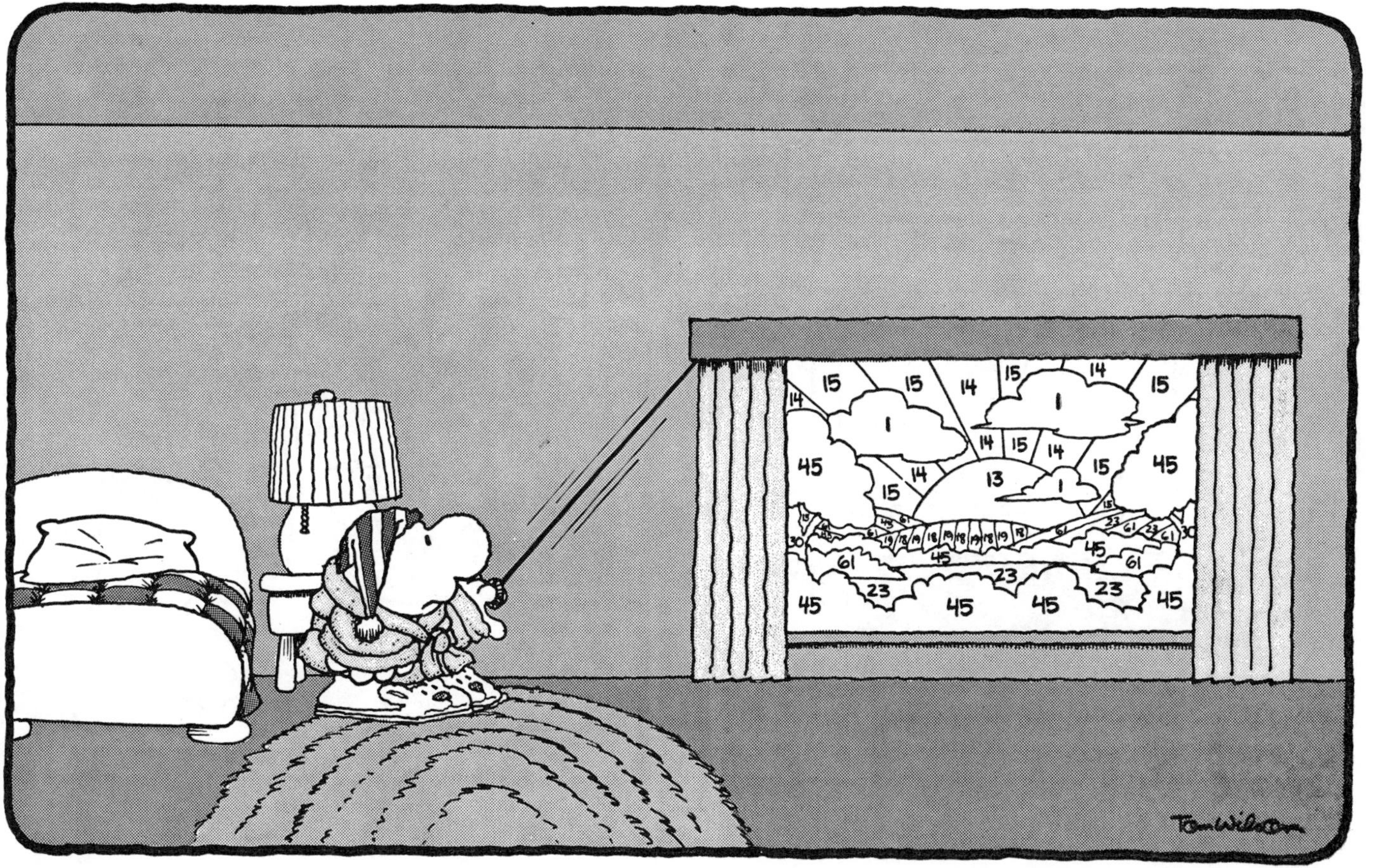
15
15
14
15
14
15
14
1
1
14
15
14
45
15
45
14
13
15
1
30
30
45
61
61
23
23
23
45
45
45
45
45

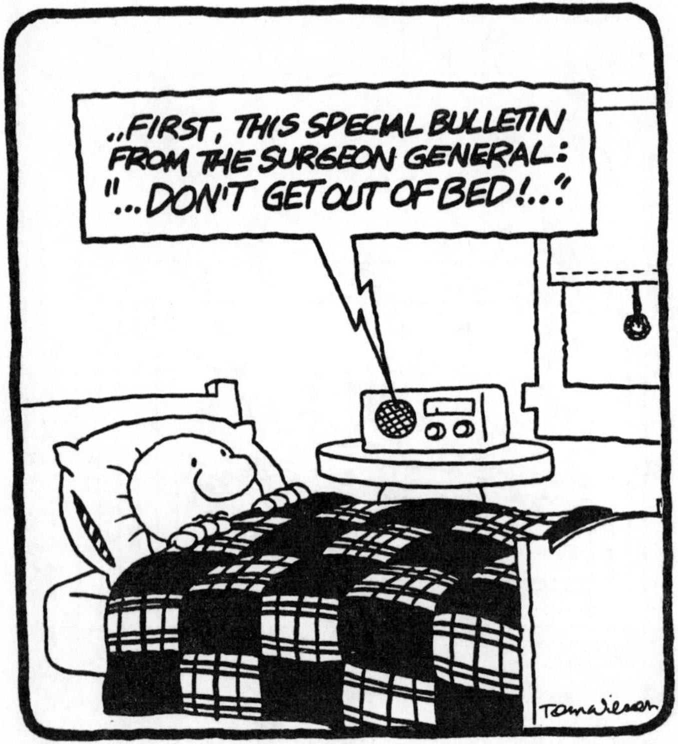
..FIRST, THIS SPECIAL BULLETIN FROM THE SURGEON GENERAL: "...DON'T GET OUT OF BED!.."
Tom Wilson

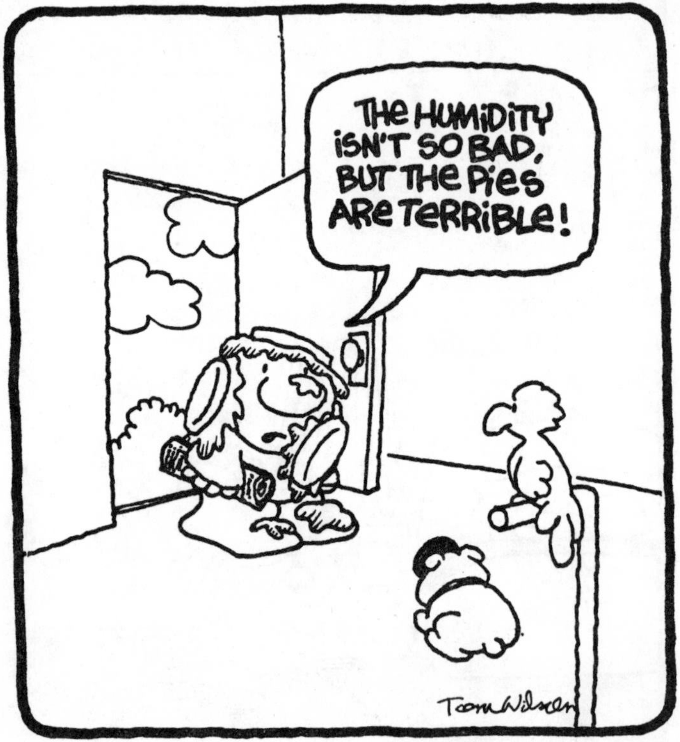
THE HUMIDITY ISN'T SO BAD, BUT THE PIES ARE TERRIBLE!
Tom Wilson

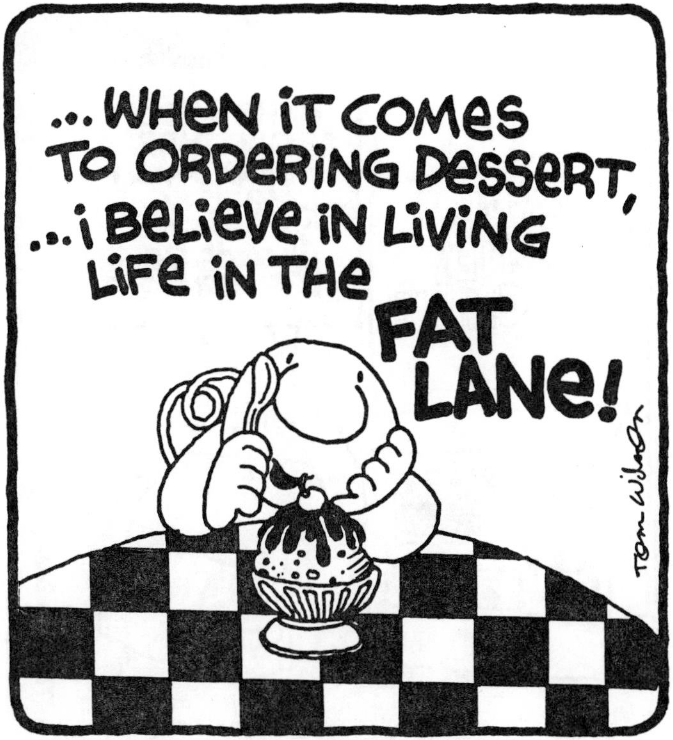
...WHEN iT COMES TO ORDERING DeSSeRT,
...i BeLieVe iN LiViNG LiFe iN THe
FAT LANe!
TOM WiLSON

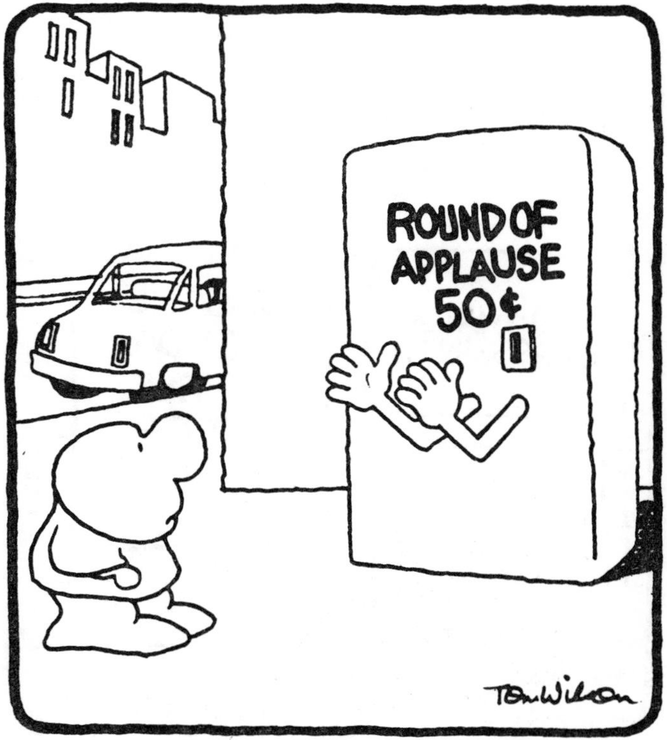
ROUND OF APPLAUSE 50¢
TOM WiLSON

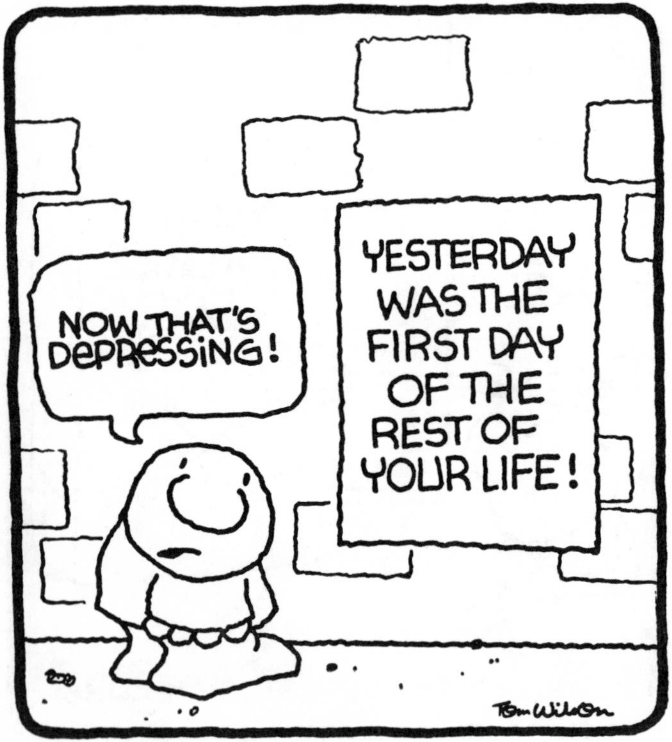
NOW THAT'S DEPRESSING!
YESTERDAY WAS THE FIRST DAY OF THE REST OF YOUR LIFE!
TOM WILSON

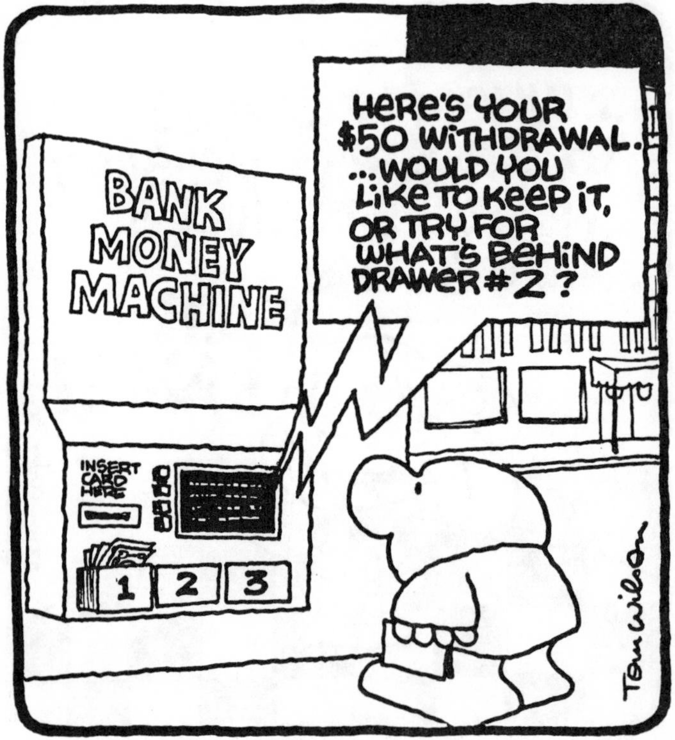
BANK MONEY MACHINE
INSERT CARD HERE
1 2 3
HERE'S YOUR $50 WITHDRAWAL. ...WOULD YOU LIKE TO KEEP IT, OR TRY FOR WHAT'S BEHIND DRAWER #2 ?
TOM WILSON

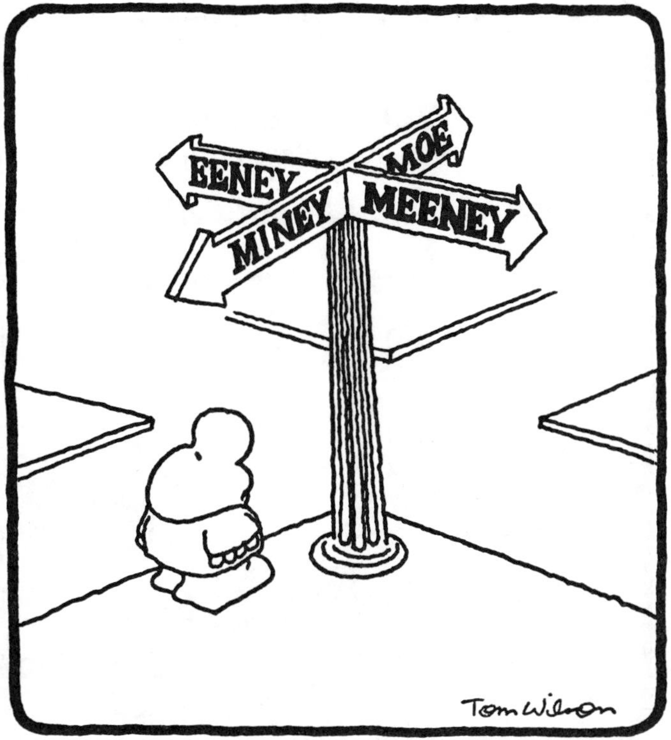

EENEY
MOE
MINEY
MEENEY
Tom Wilson

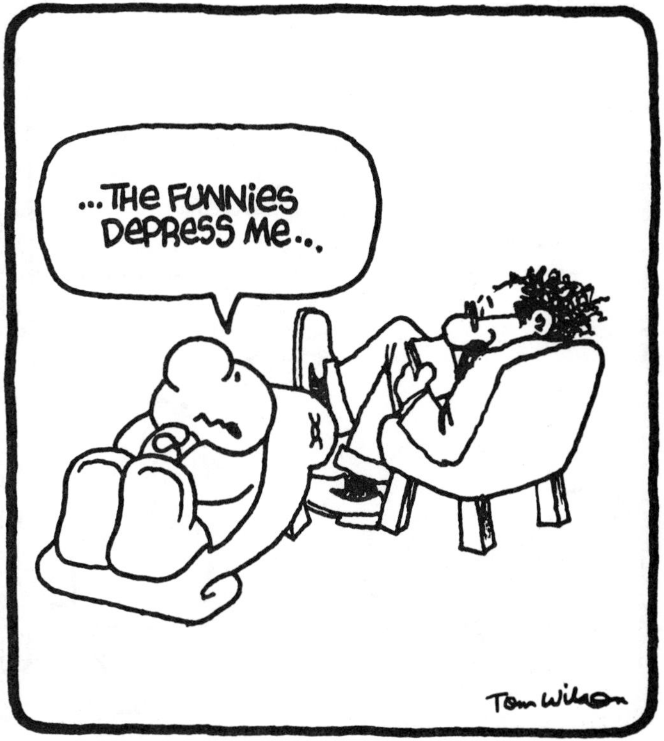

...THE FUNNIES DEPRESS ME...
Tom Wilson

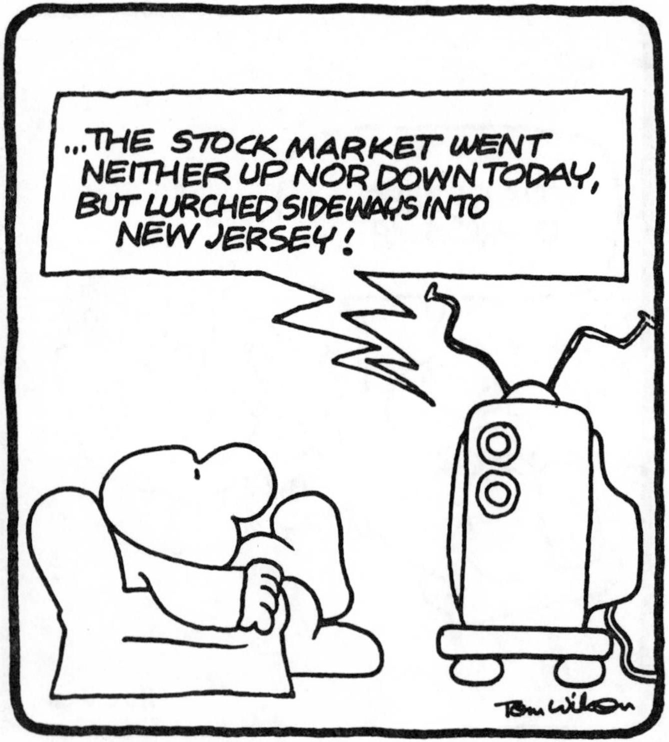
...THE STOCK MARKET WENT NEITHER UP NOR DOWN TODAY, BUT LURCHED SIDEWAYS INTO NEW JERSEY!
TOM WILSON

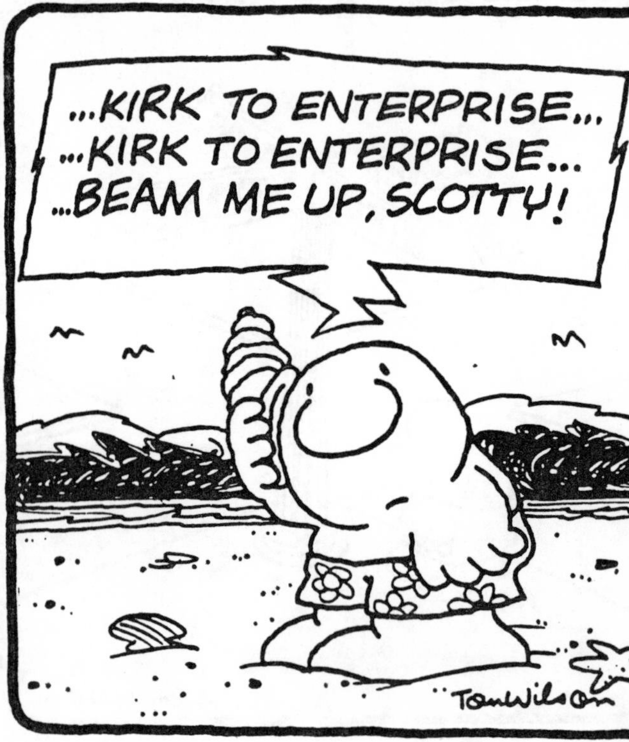
...KIRK TO ENTERPRISE... ...KIRK TO ENTERPRISE... ...BEAM ME UP, SCOTTY!
TOM WILSON

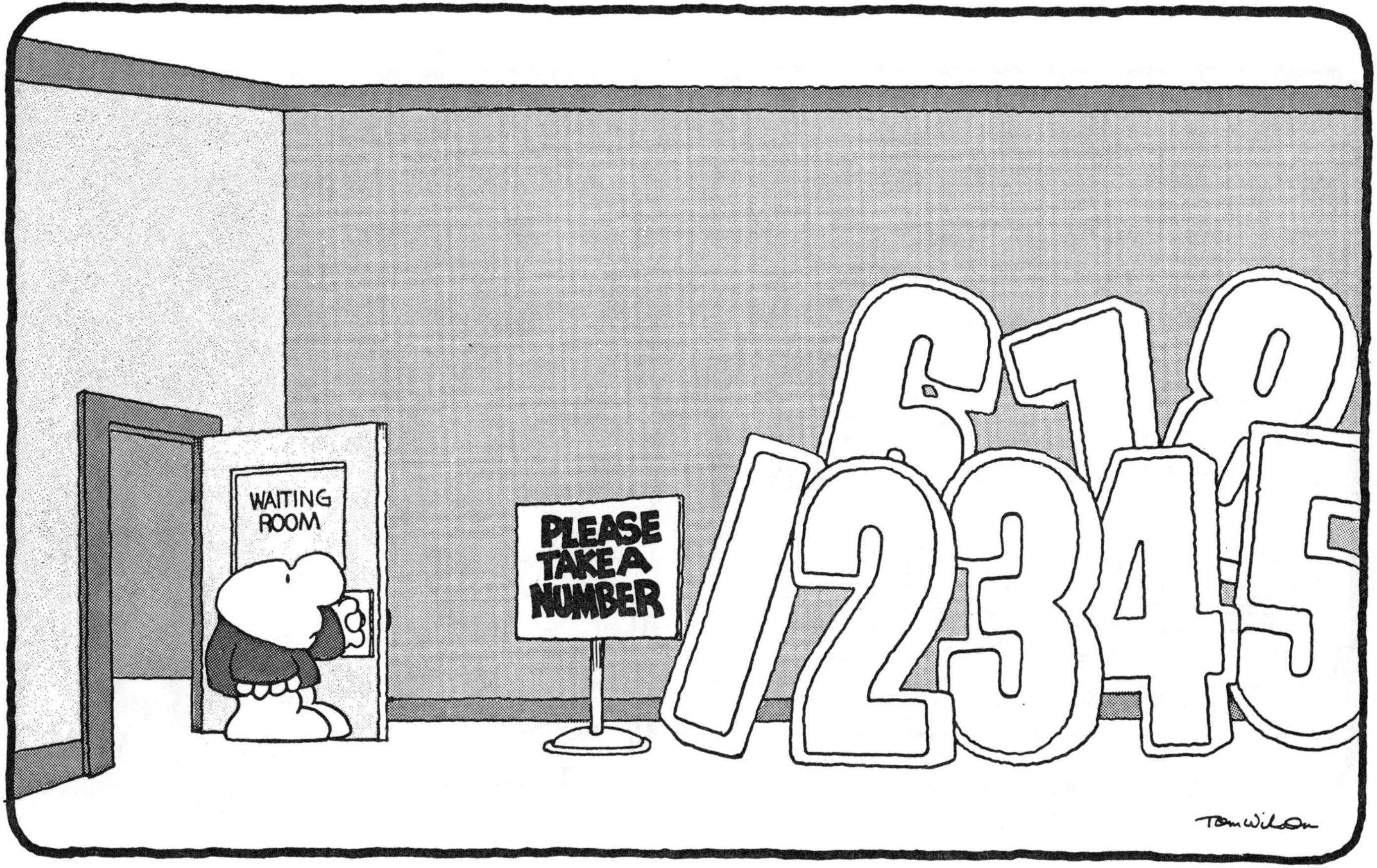
WAITING ROOM
PLEASE TAKE A NUMBER
12345
678
Tom Wilson

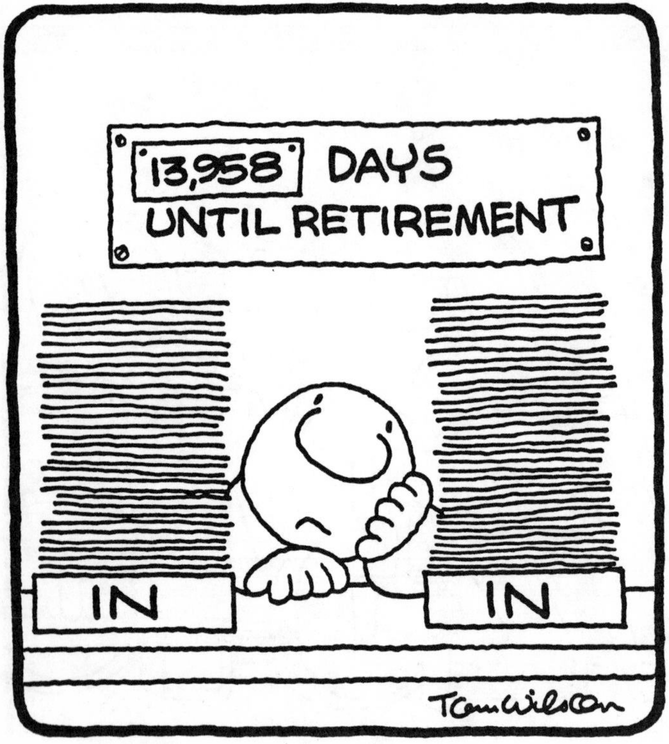
13,958 DAYS
UNTIL RETIREMENT
IN
IN
Tom Wilson

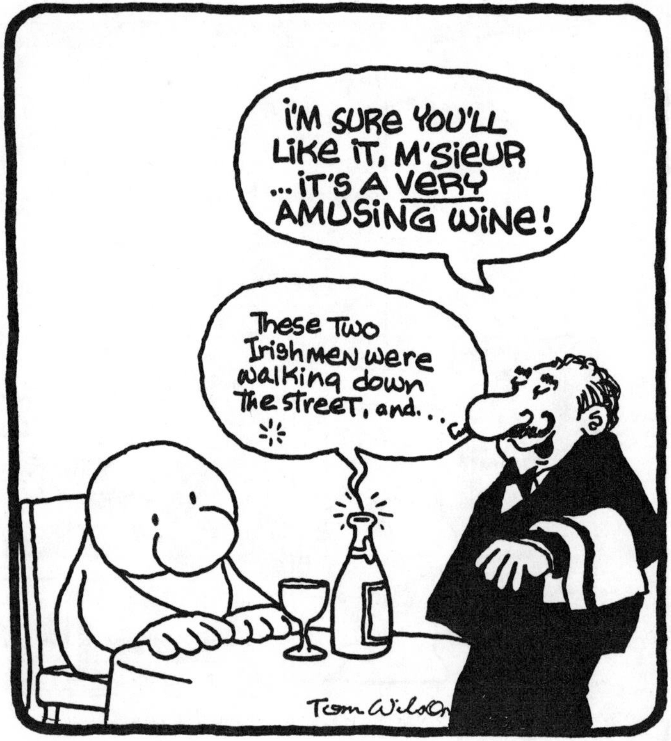
I'M SURE YOU'LL LIKE IT, M'SIEUR ... IT'S A VERY AMUSING WINE!
These Two Irishmen were walking down The street, and...
Tom Wilson

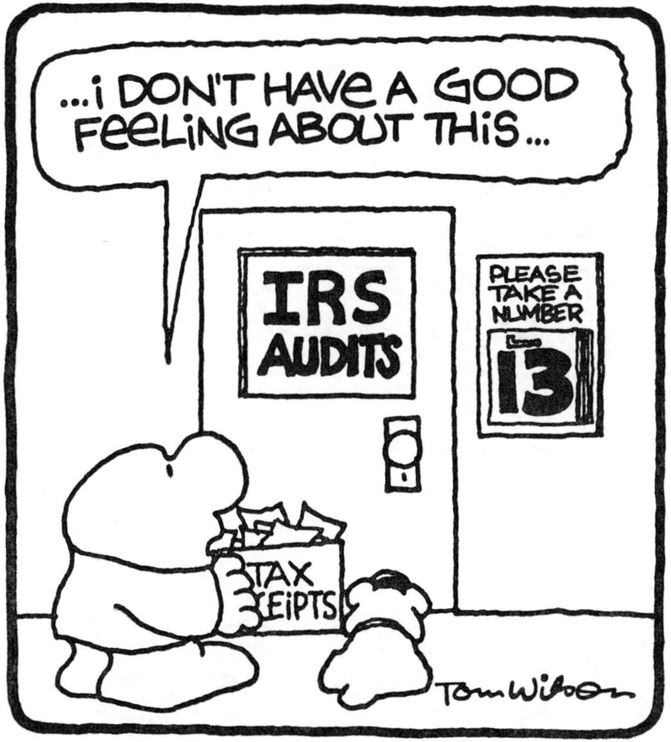
...i DON'T HAVE A GOOD FEELiNG ABOUT THiS...
IRS AUDITS
PLEASE TAKE A NUMBER
13
TAX
EIPTS
Tom Wilson

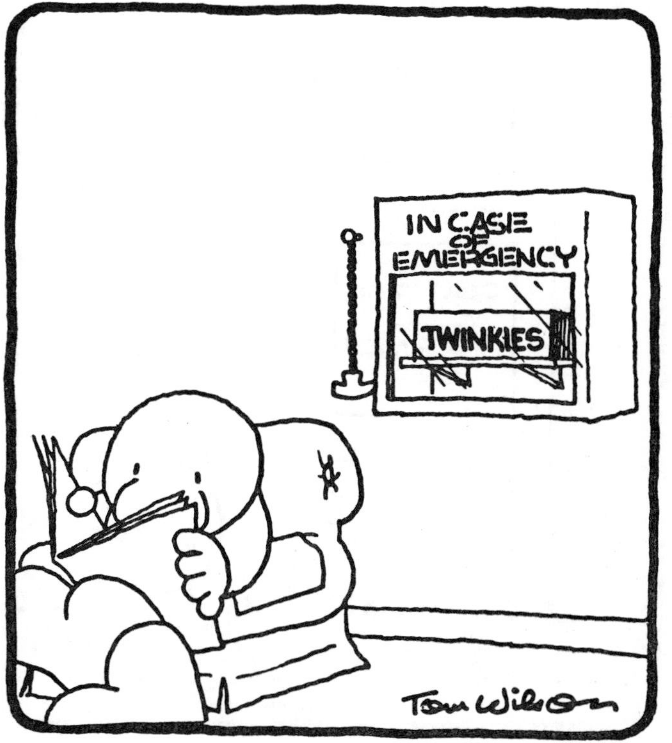
IN CASE OF EMERGENCY
TWINKIES
Tom Wilson

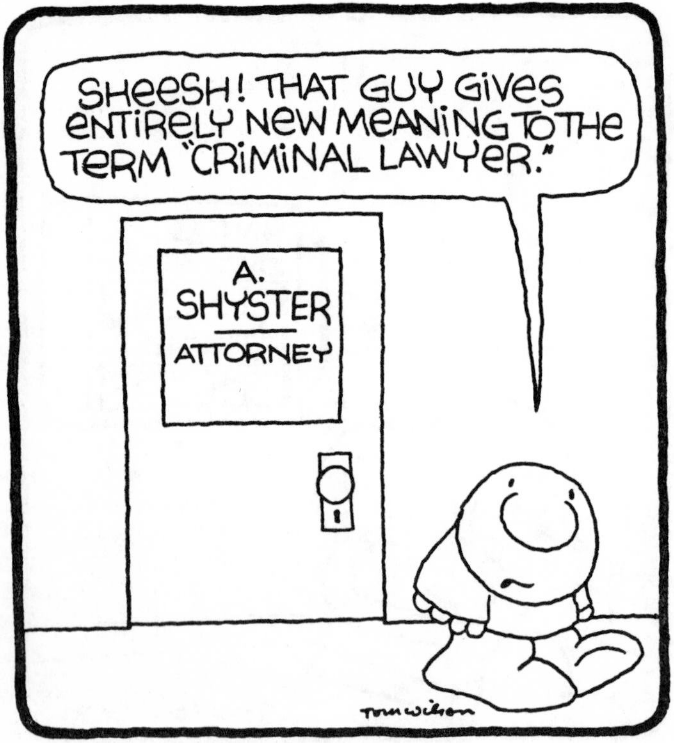
SHEESH! THAT GUY GIVES ENTIRELY NEW MEANING TO THE TERM "CRIMINAL LAWYER."
A. SHYSTER
ATTORNEY
TOM WILSON

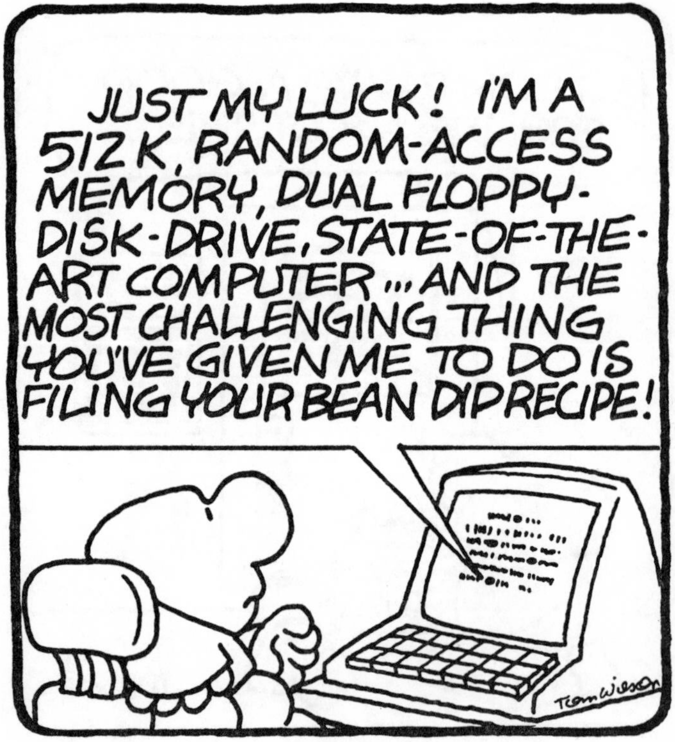
JUST MY LUCK! I'M A 512K, RANDOM-ACCESS MEMORY, DUAL FLOPPY-DISK-DRIVE, STATE-OF-THE-ART COMPUTER ... AND THE MOST CHALLENGING THING YOU'VE GIVEN ME TO DO IS FILING YOUR BEAN DIP RECIPE!
TOM WILSON

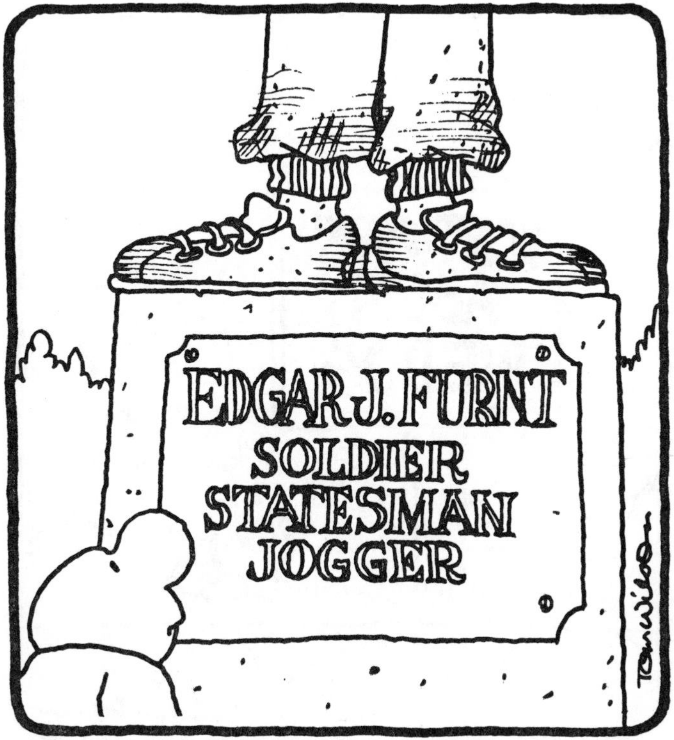
EDGAR J. FURNT
SOLDIER
STATESMAN
JOGGER
Tom Wilson

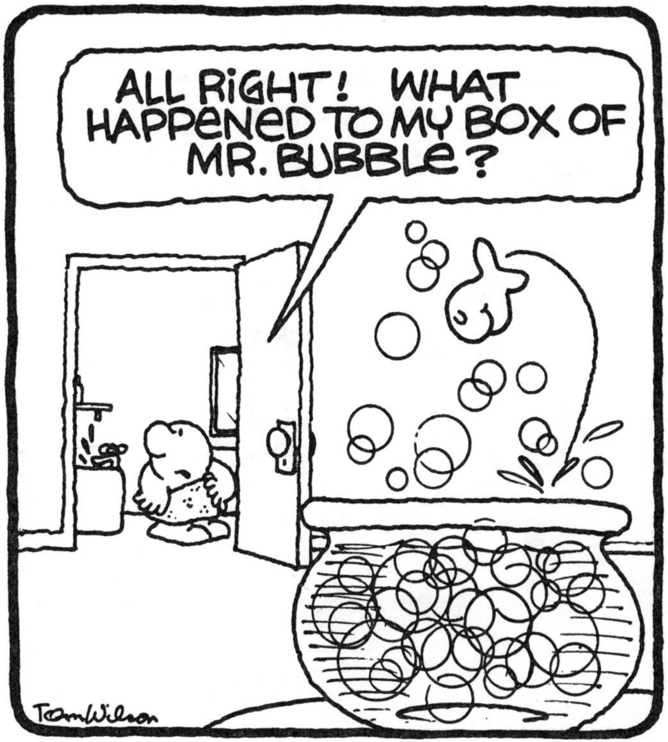
ALL RIGHT! WHAT HAPPENED TO MY BOX OF MR. BUBBLE?
Tom Wilson

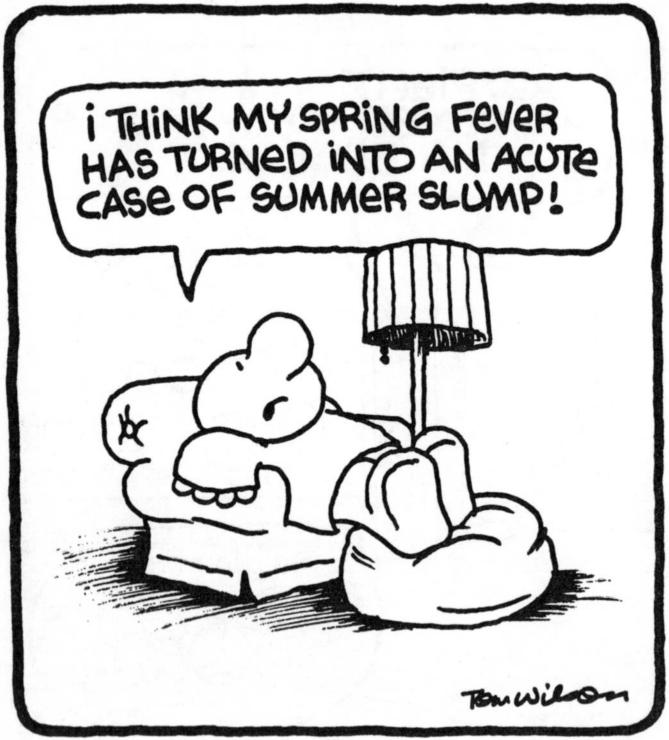
I THINK MY SPRING FEVER HAS TURNED INTO AN ACUTE CASE OF SUMMER SLUMP!
Tom Wilson

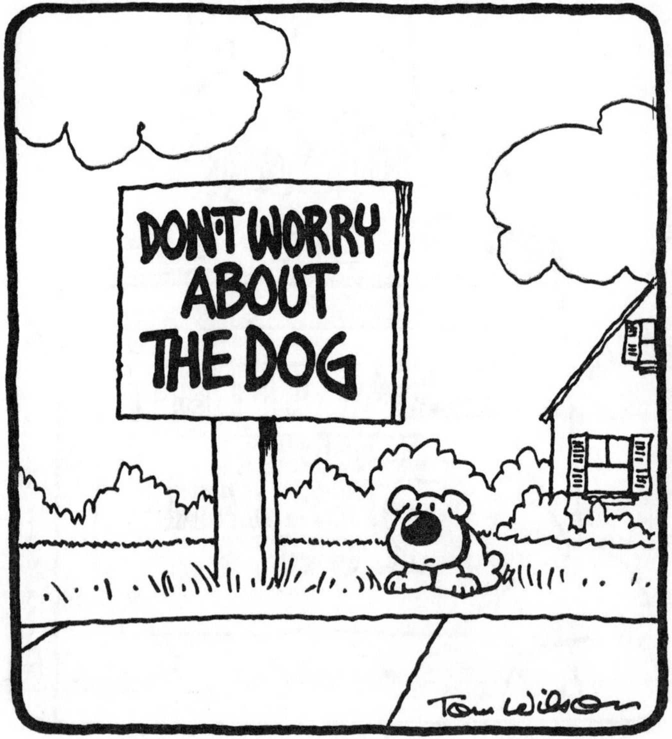
DON'T WORRY ABOUT THE DOG
Tom Wilson

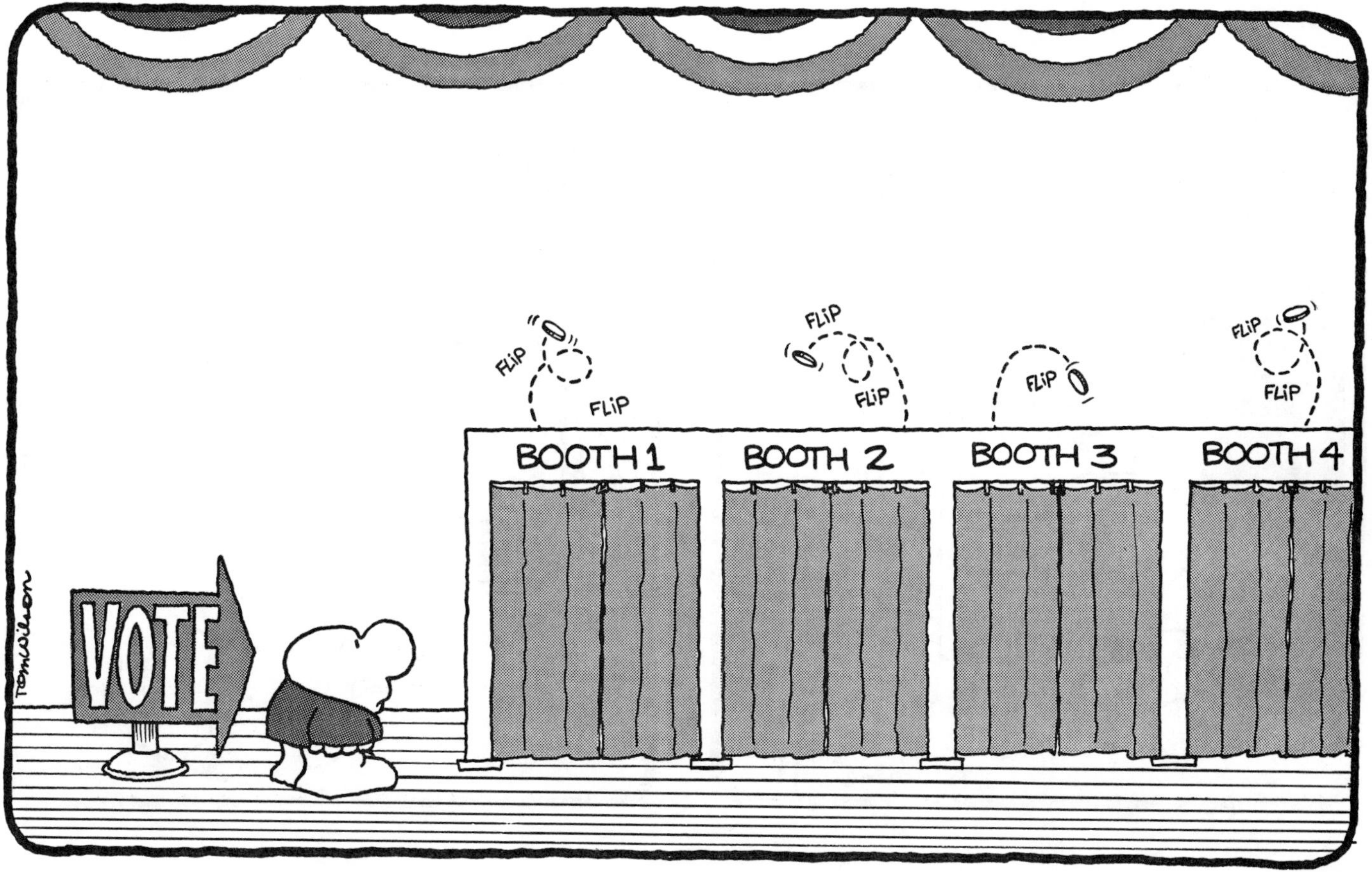
VOTE
BOOTH 1
BOOTH 2
BOOTH 3
BOOTH 4
FLIP
FLIP
FLIP
FLIP
FLIP
FLIP
FLIP
FLIP
tomwilson

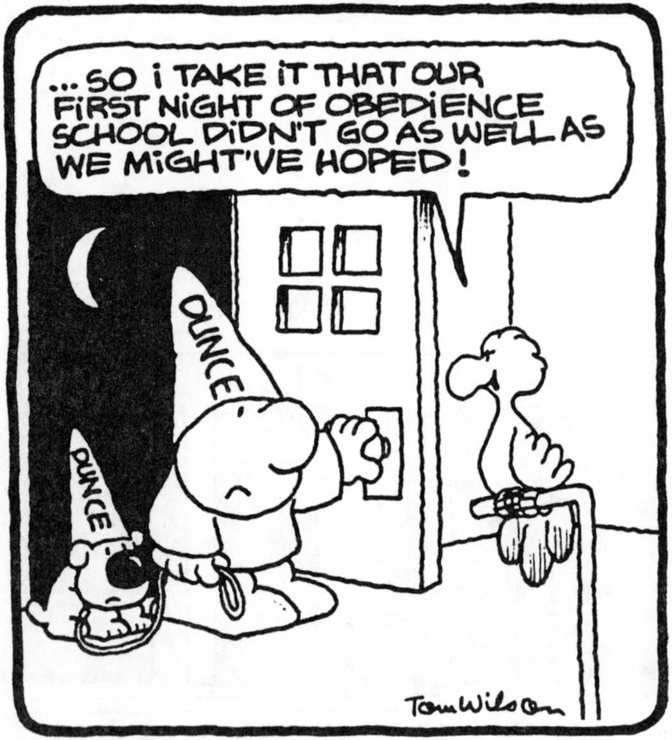
...SO I TAKE IT THAT OUR FIRST NIGHT OF OBEDIENCE SCHOOL DIDN'T GO AS WELL AS WE MIGHT'VE HOPED!
DUNCE
DUNCE
Tom Wilson

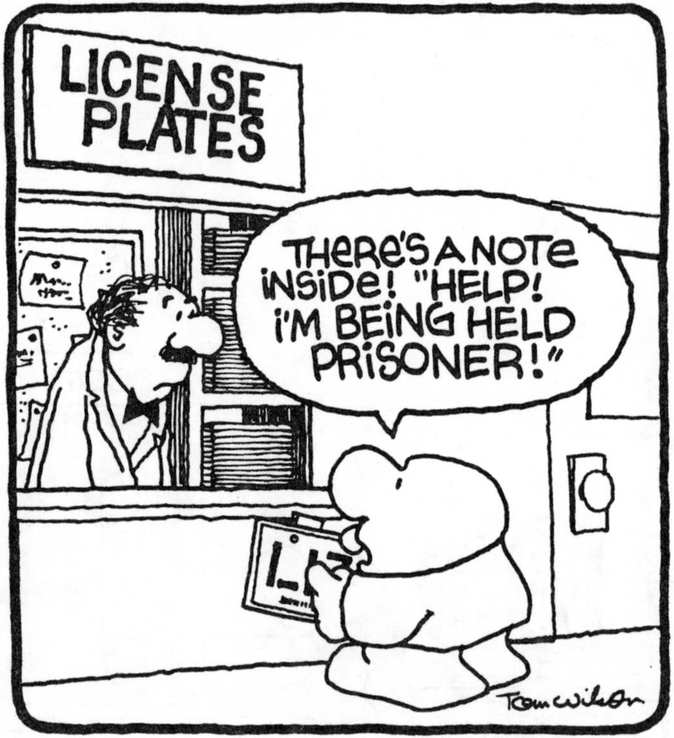
LICENSE PLATES
THERE'S A NOTE INSIDE! "HELP! I'M BEING HELD PRISONER!"
Tom Wilson

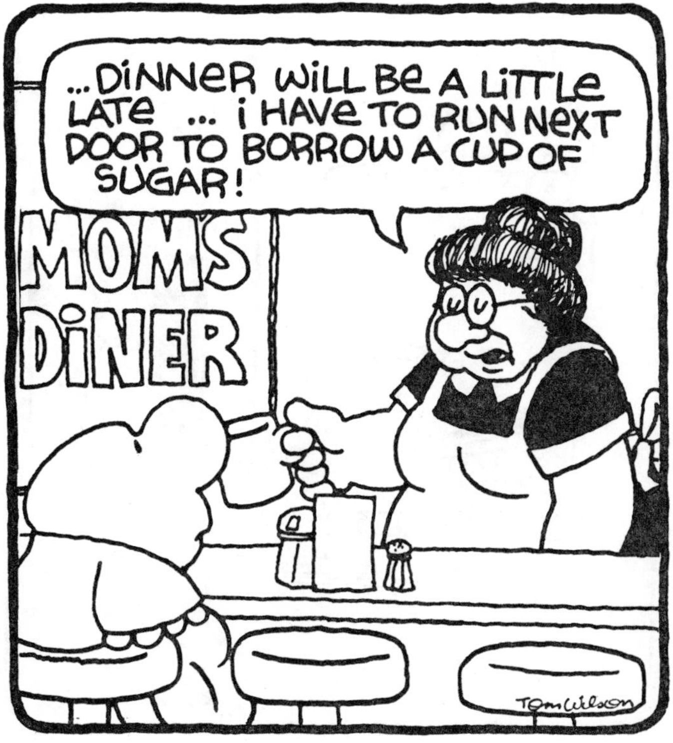
...DINNER WILL BE A LITTLE LATE ... I HAVE TO RUN NEXT DOOR TO BORROW A CUP OF SUGAR!
MOM'S DINER
Tom Wilson

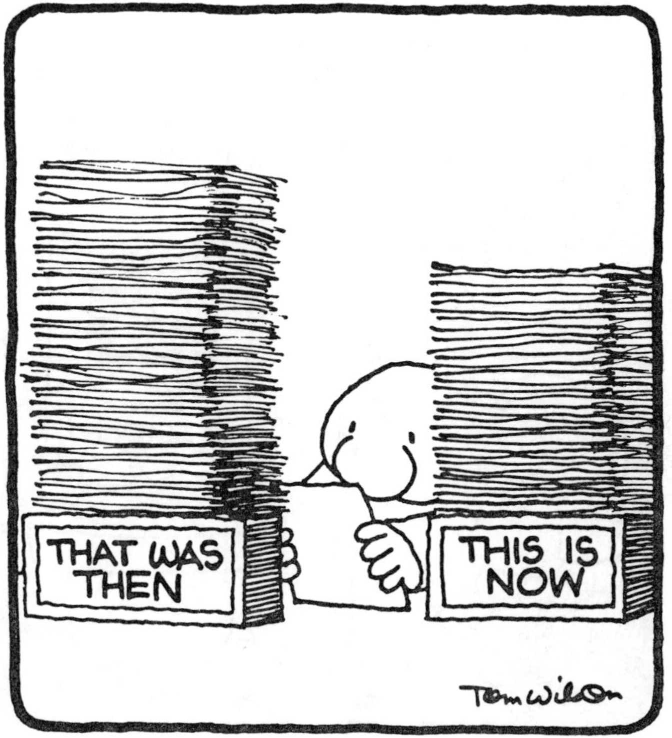
THAT WAS THEN
THIS IS NOW
Tom Wilson

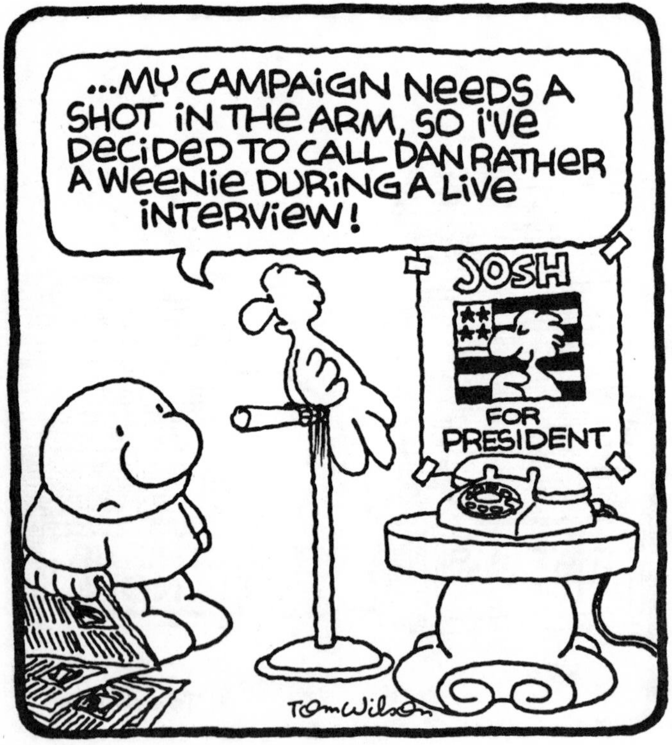
...MY CAMPAIGN NEEDS A SHOT IN THE ARM, SO I'VE DECIDED TO CALL DAN RATHER A WEENIE DURING A LIVE INTERVIEW!
JOSH
FOR PRESIDENT
TOM WILSON

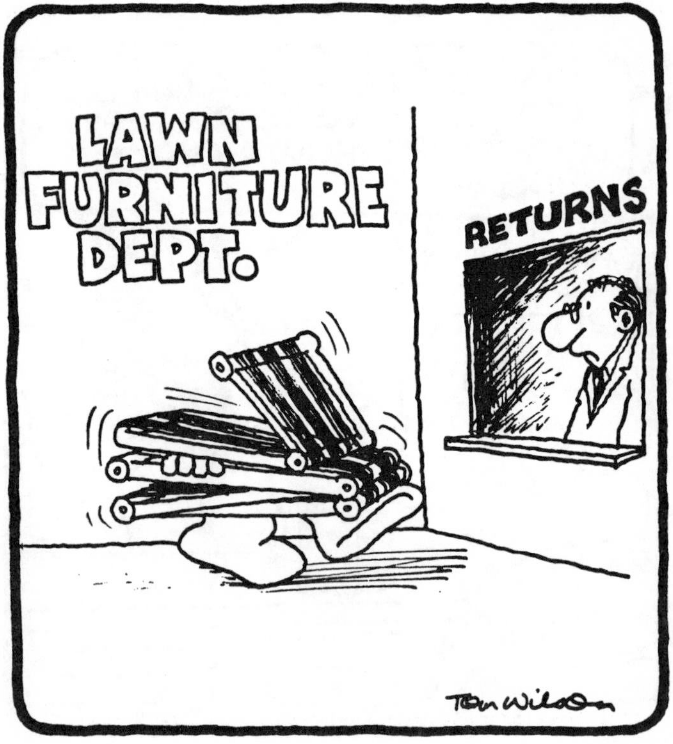
LAWN FURNITURE DEPT.
RETURNS
TOM WILSON

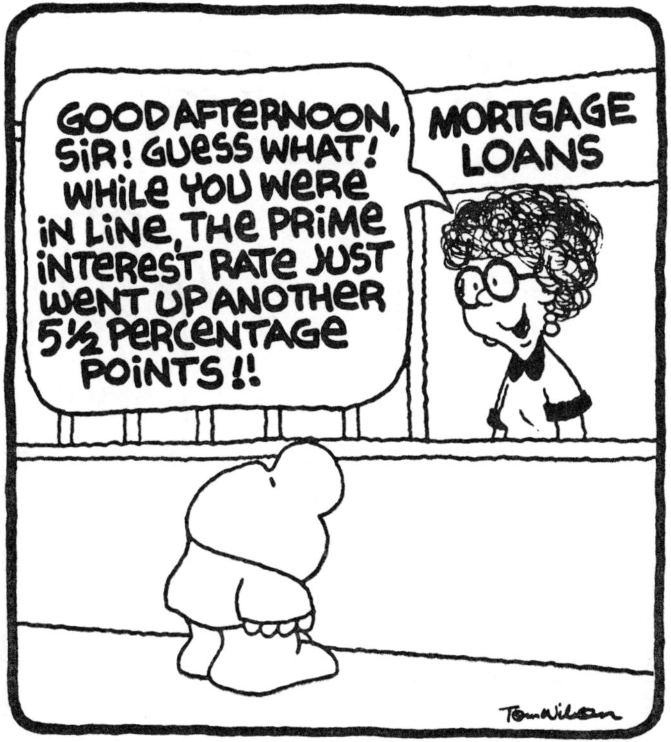
GOOD AFTERNOON, SIR! GUESS WHAT! WHILE YOU WERE IN LINE, THE PRIME INTEREST RATE JUST WENT UP ANOTHER 5½ PERCENTAGE POINTS!!
MORTGAGE LOANS
Tom Wilson

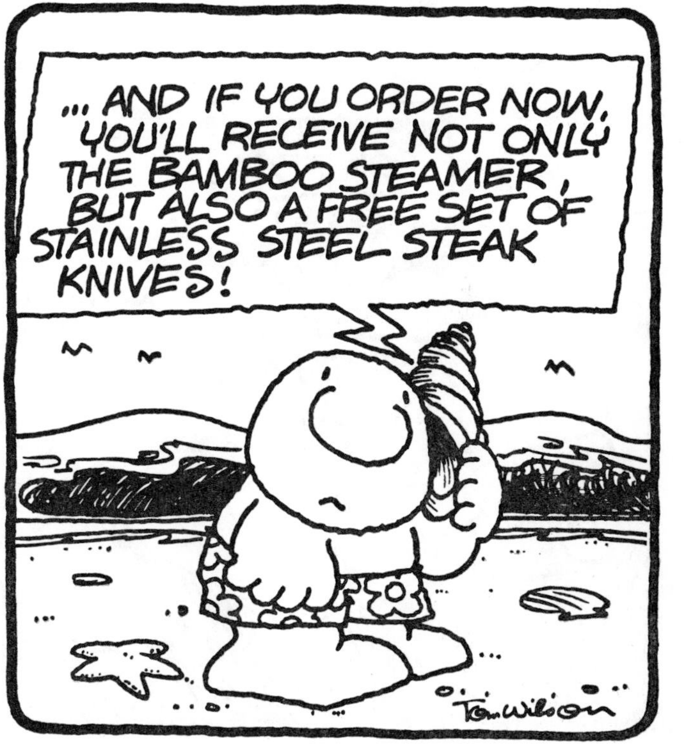
... AND IF YOU ORDER NOW, YOU'LL RECEIVE NOT ONLY THE BAMBOO STEAMER, BUT ALSO A FREE SET OF STAINLESS STEEL STEAK KNIVES!
Tom Wilson

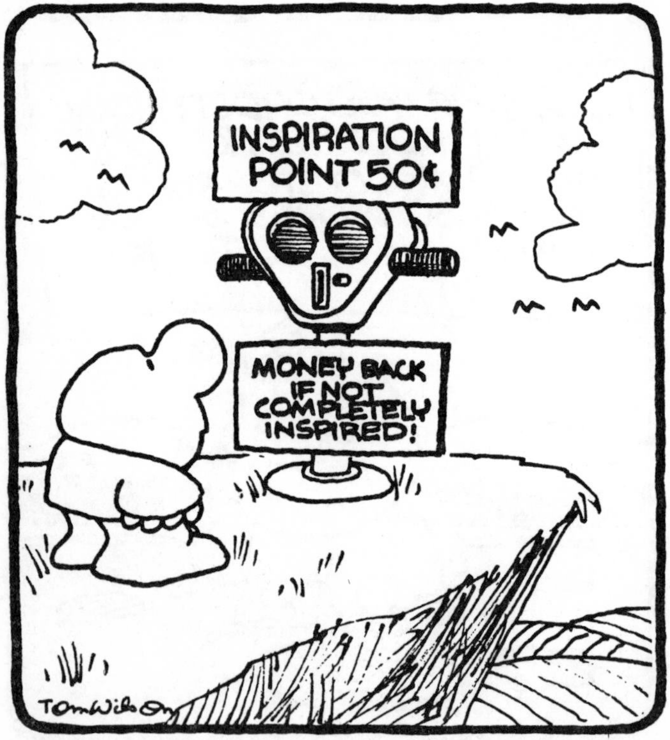
INSPIRATION POINT 50¢
MONEY BACK IF NOT COMPLETELY INSPIRED!
TOM WILSON

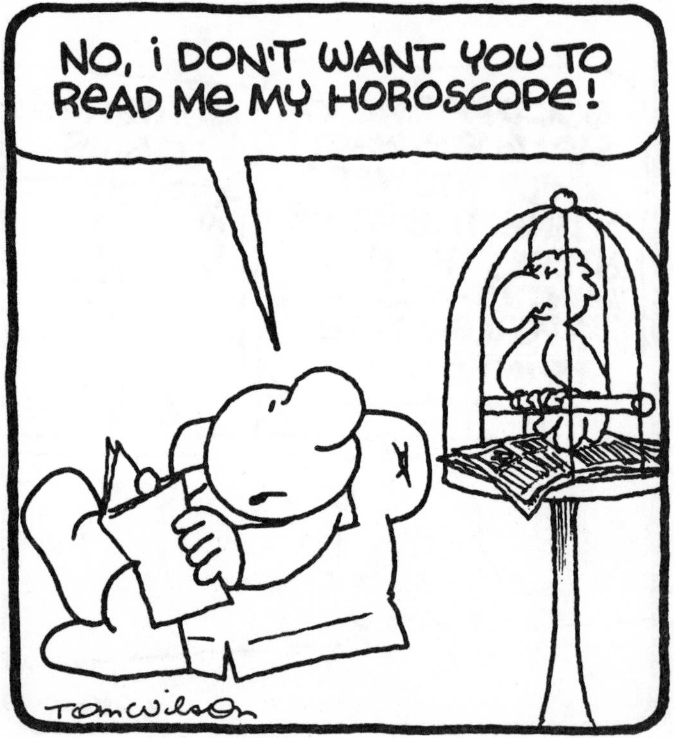
NO, i DON'T WANT YOU TO READ ME MY HOROSCOPE!
TOM WILSON

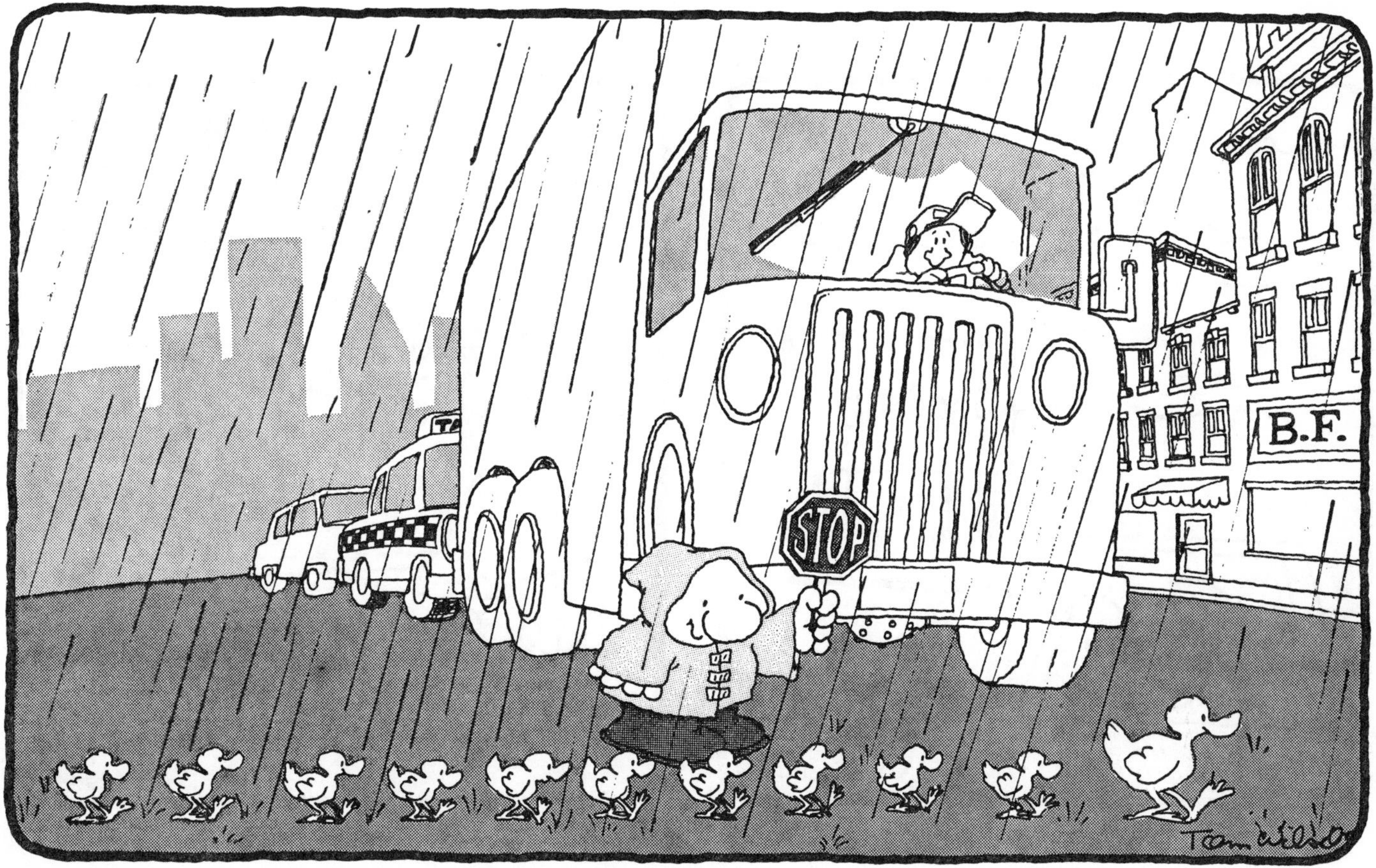
STOP
B.F.
Tom Wilson

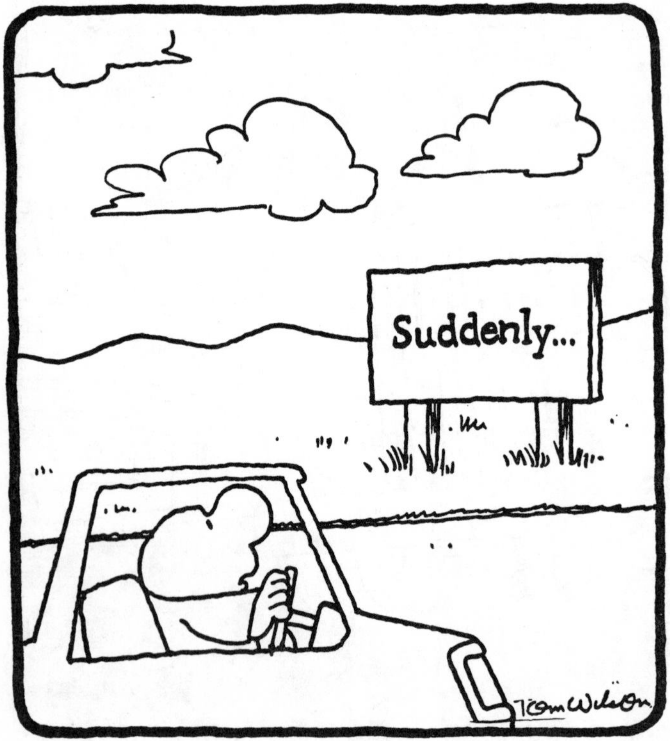
Suddenly...
TomWilson

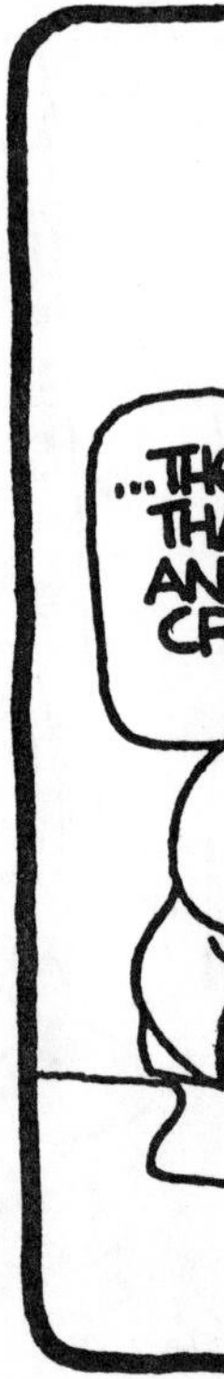
INFORMATION
...THEN YOU FLIP THAT END UP AND OVER THE CRISSCROSSED PART..
TomWilson

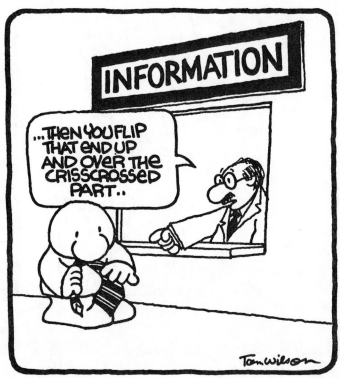

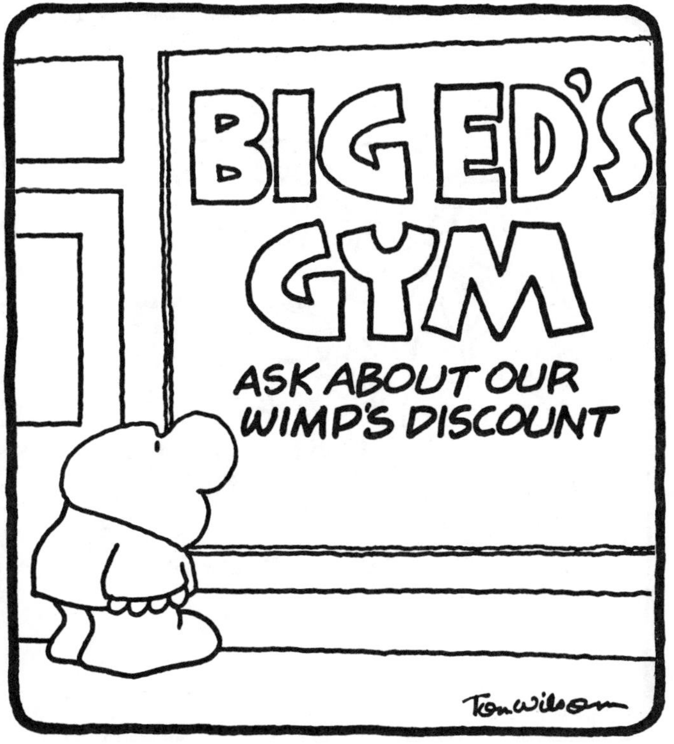
BIG ED'S GYM
ASK ABOUT OUR WIMP'S DISCOUNT
Tom Wilson

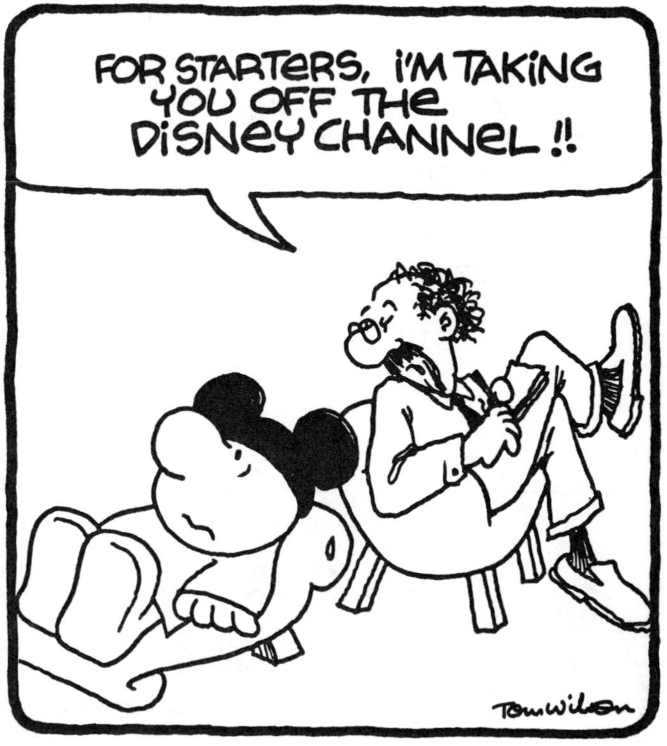
FOR STARTERS, I'M TAKING YOU OFF THE DISNEY CHANNEL !!
Tom Wilson

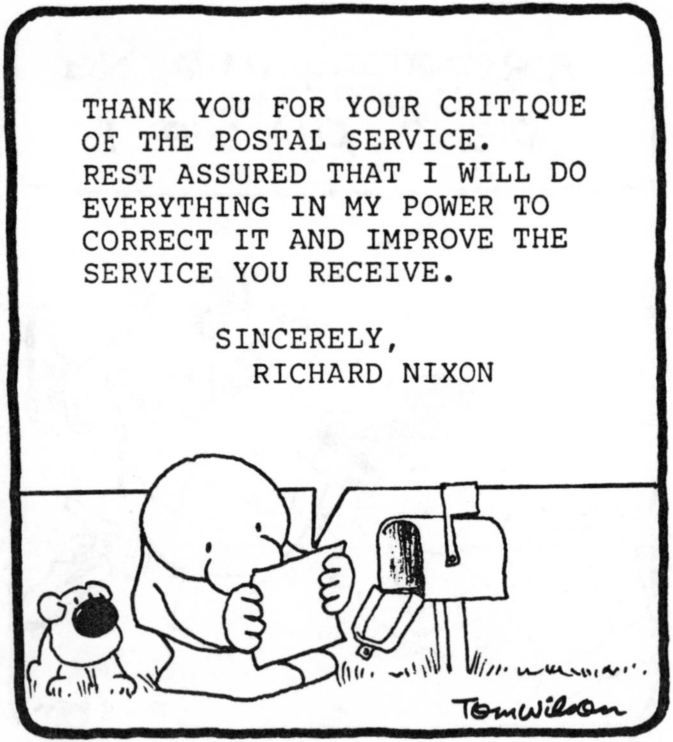
THANK YOU FOR YOUR CRITIQUE OF THE POSTAL SERVICE. REST ASSURED THAT I WILL DO EVERYTHING IN MY POWER TO CORRECT IT AND IMPROVE THE SERVICE YOU RECEIVE.
SINCERELY,
RICHARD NIXON
Tom Wilson

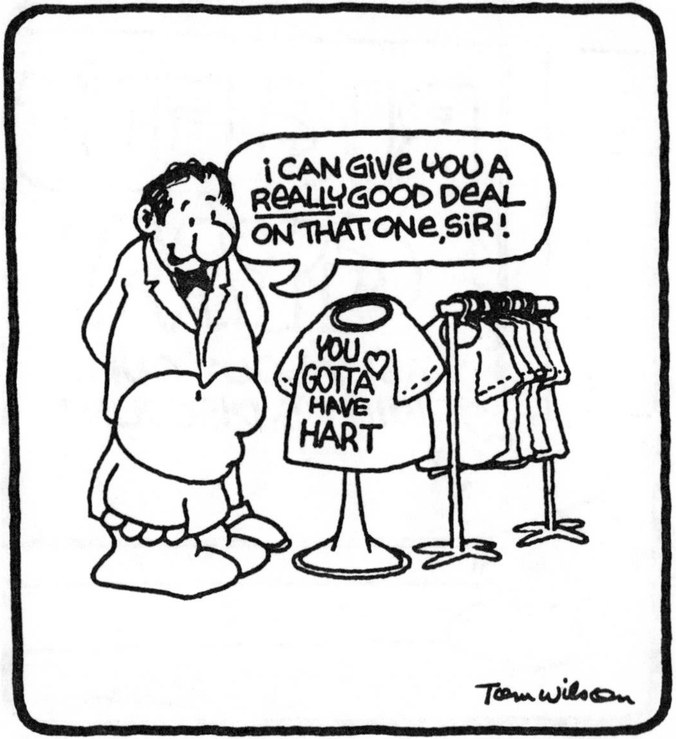
I CAN GIVE YOU A REALLY GOOD DEAL ON THAT ONE, SIR!
YOU ♡ GOTTA HAVE HART
Tom Wilson

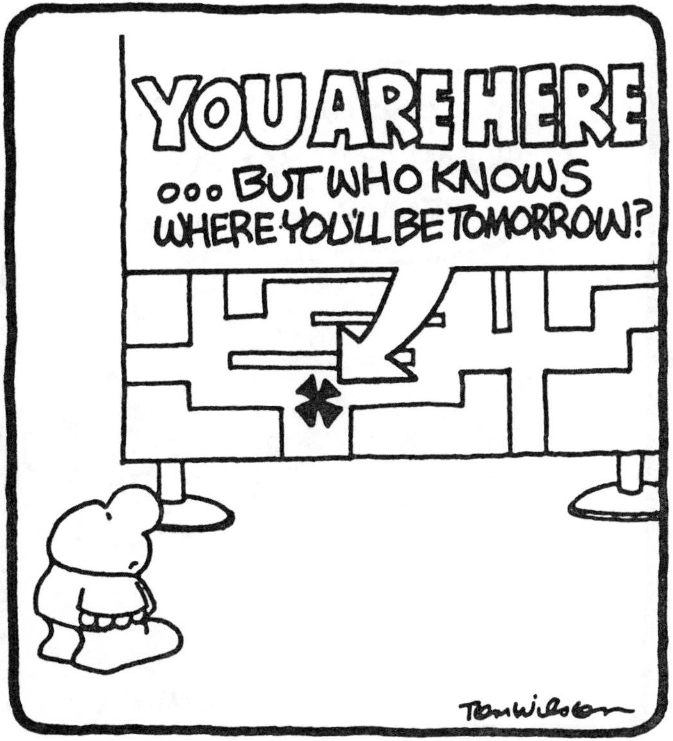
YOU ARE HERE
... BUT WHO KNOWS WHERE YOU'LL BE TOMORROW?
Tom Wilson

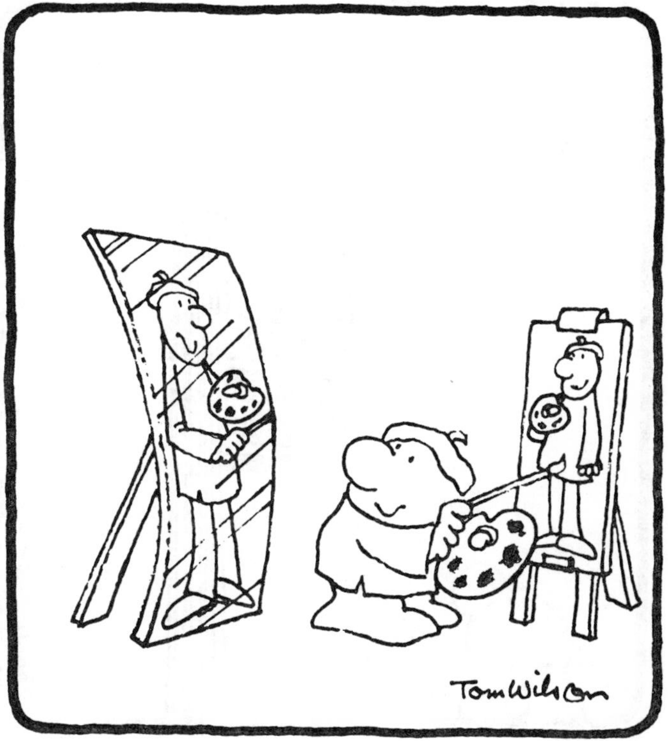
Tom Wilson

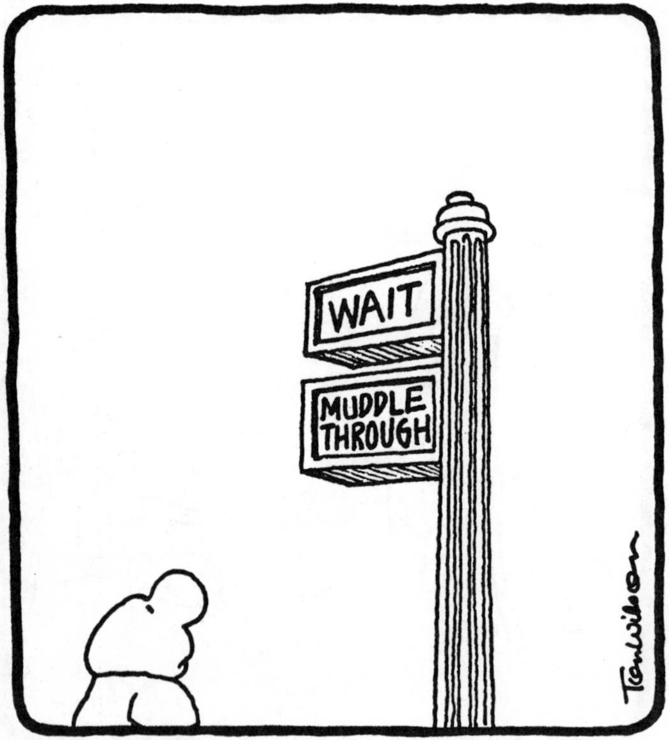
WAIT
MUDDLE THROUGH
Tom Wilson

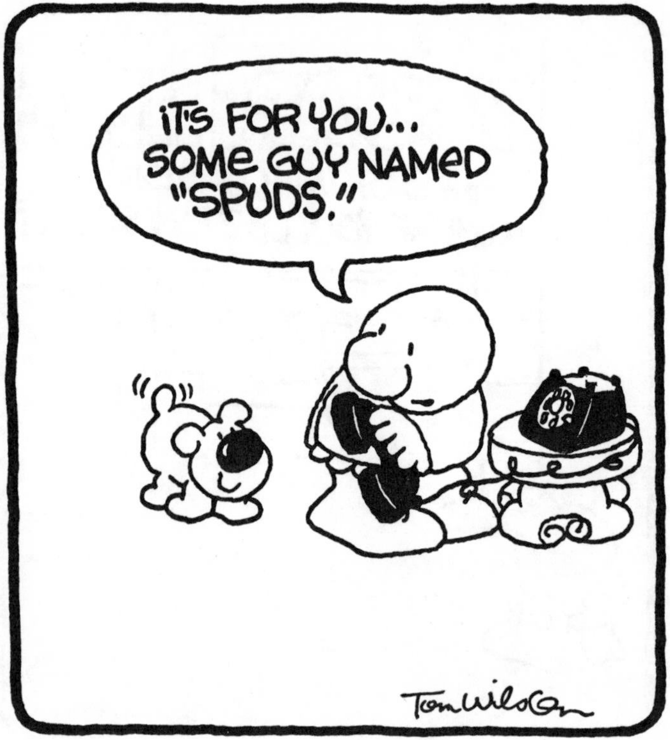
IT'S FOR YOU... SOME GUY NAMED "SPUDS."
Tom Wilson

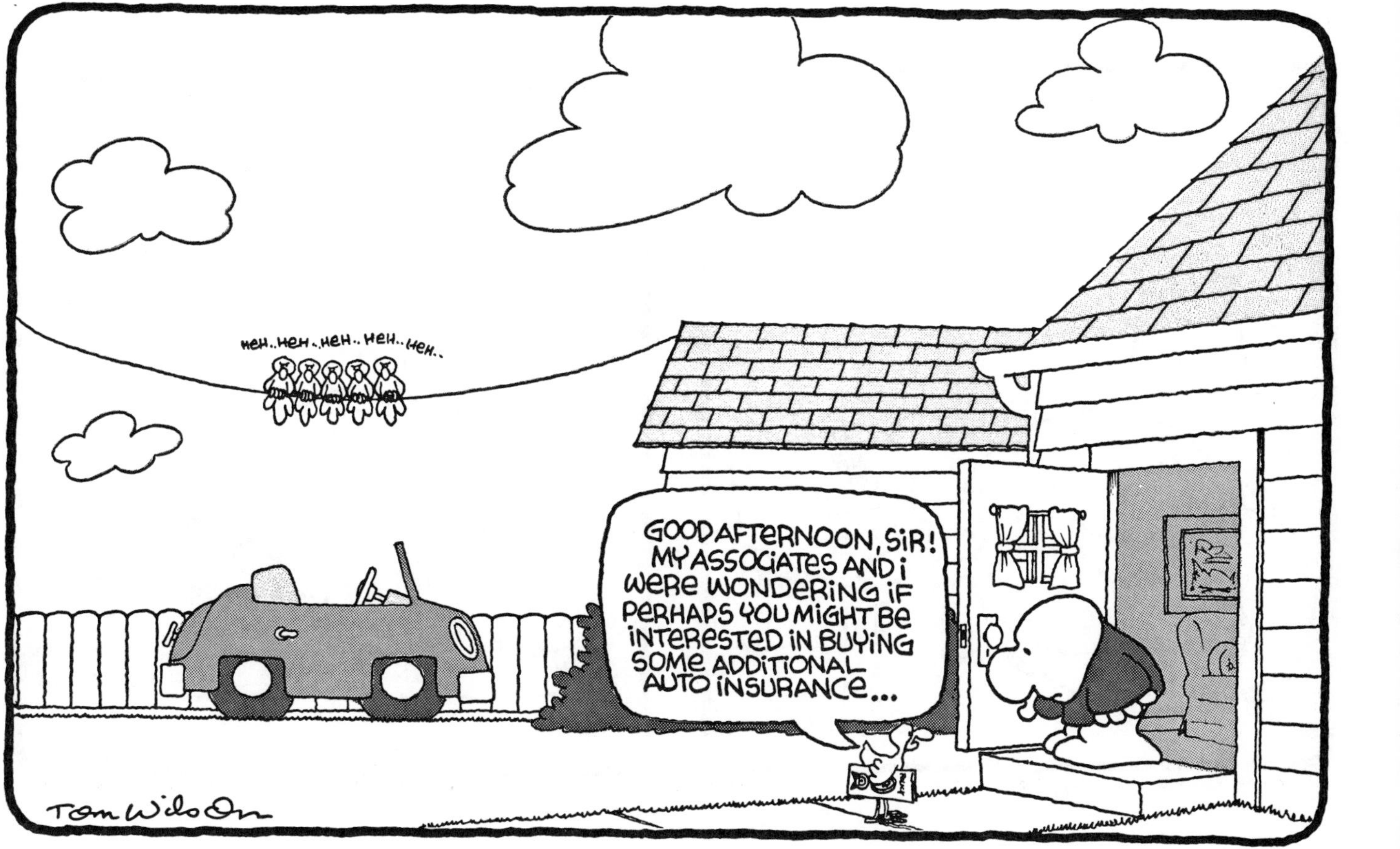
HEH.. HEH.. HEH.. HEH.. HEH..
GOOD AFTERNOON, SIR! MY ASSOCIATES AND I WERE WONDERING IF PERHAPS YOU MIGHT BE INTERESTED IN BUYING SOME ADDITIONAL AUTO INSURANCE...
TOM WILSON

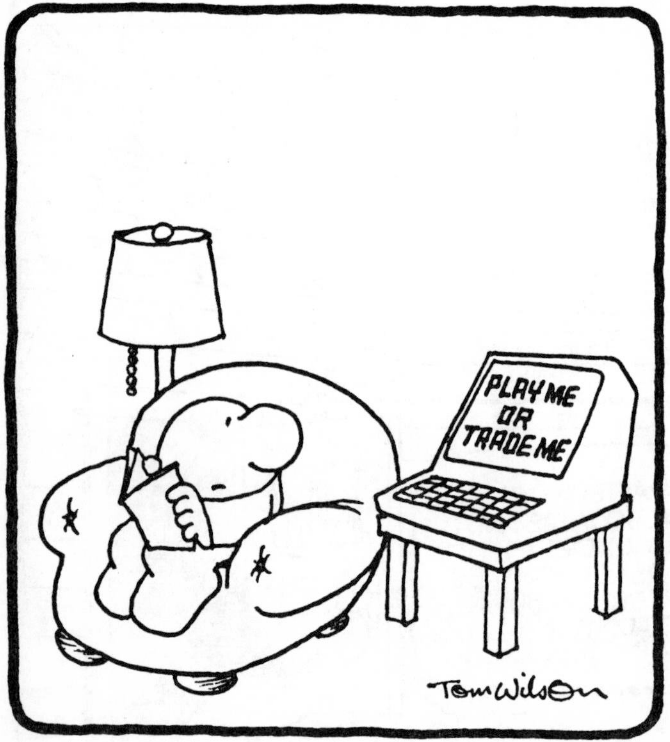
PLAY ME
OR
TRADE ME
TomWilson

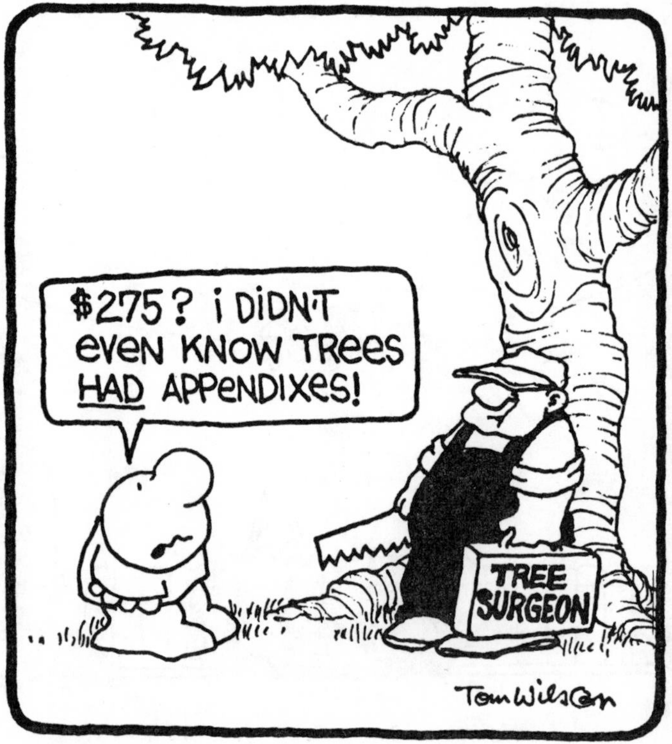
$275 ? i DIDN'T even KNOW TRees HAD APPenDIXes!
TREE SURGEON
TomWilson

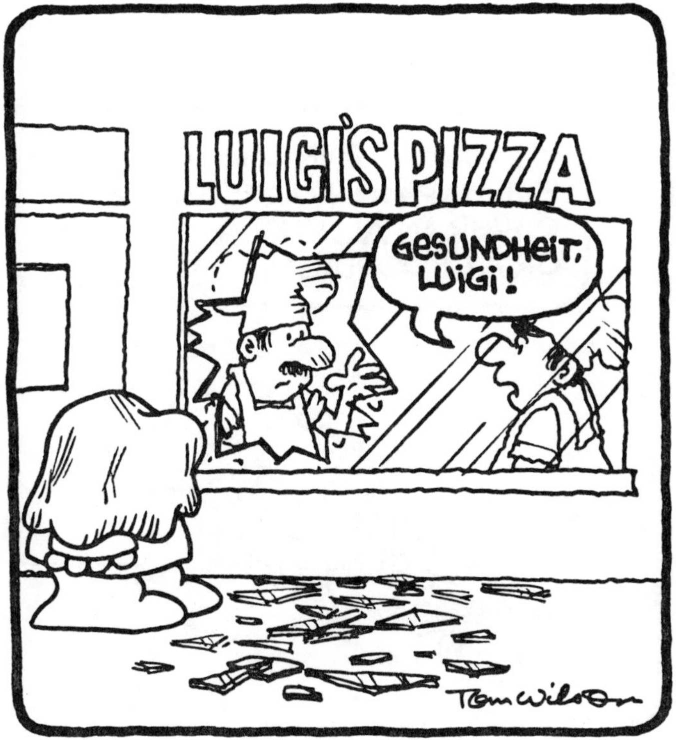
LUIGI'S PIZZA
GESUNDHEIT, LUIGI!
Tom Wilson

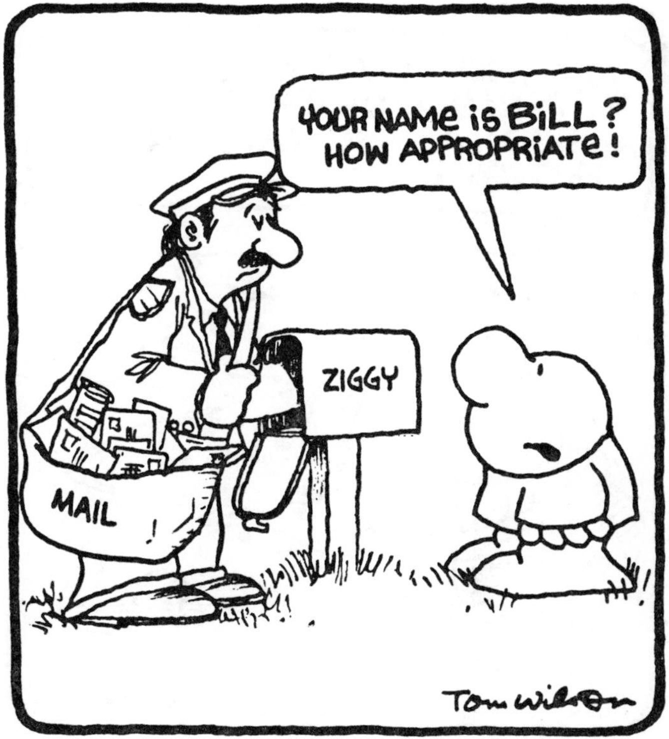
YOUR NAME IS BILL? HOW APPROPRIATE!
ZIGGY
MAIL
Tom Wilson

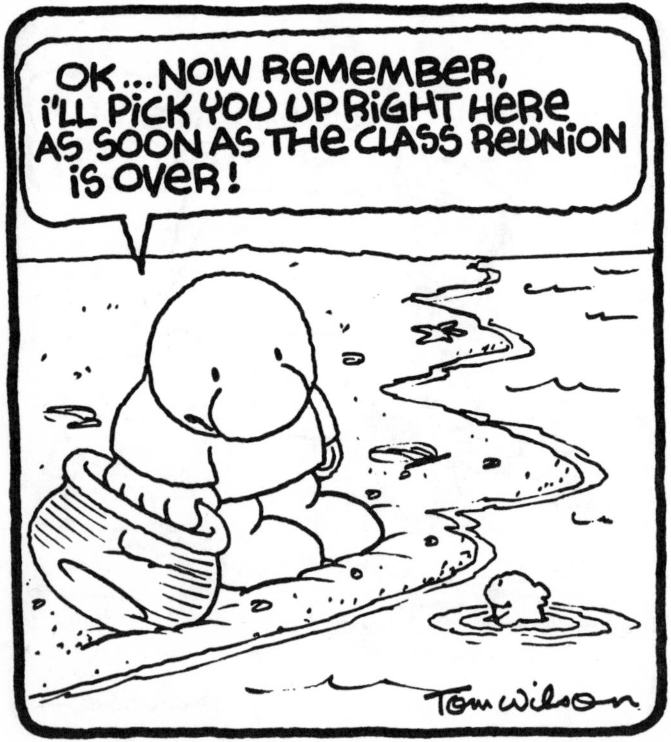
OK... NOW REMEMBER, I'LL PICK YOU UP RIGHT HERE AS SOON AS THE CLASS REUNION IS OVER!
Tom Wilson

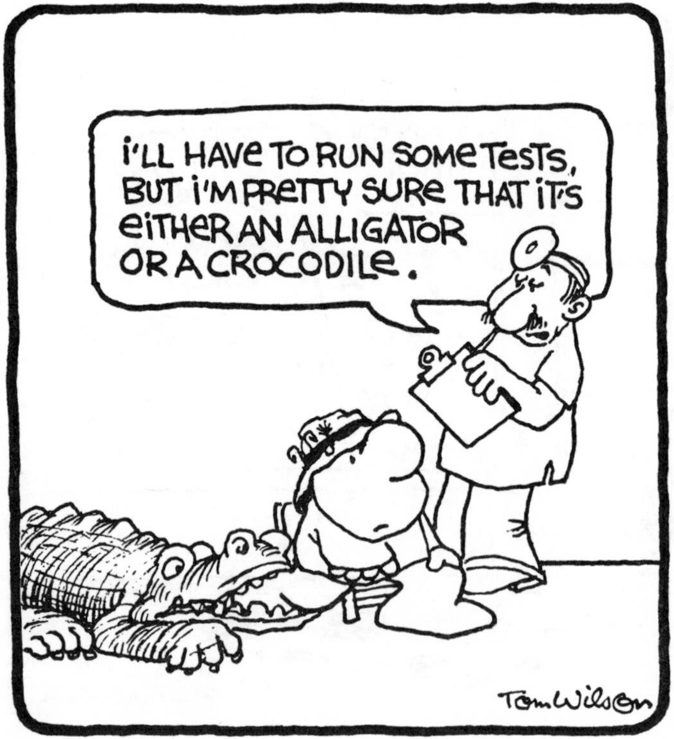
I'LL HAVE TO RUN SOME TESTS, BUT I'M PRETTY SURE THAT IT'S EITHER AN ALLIGATOR OR A CROCODILE.
Tom Wilson

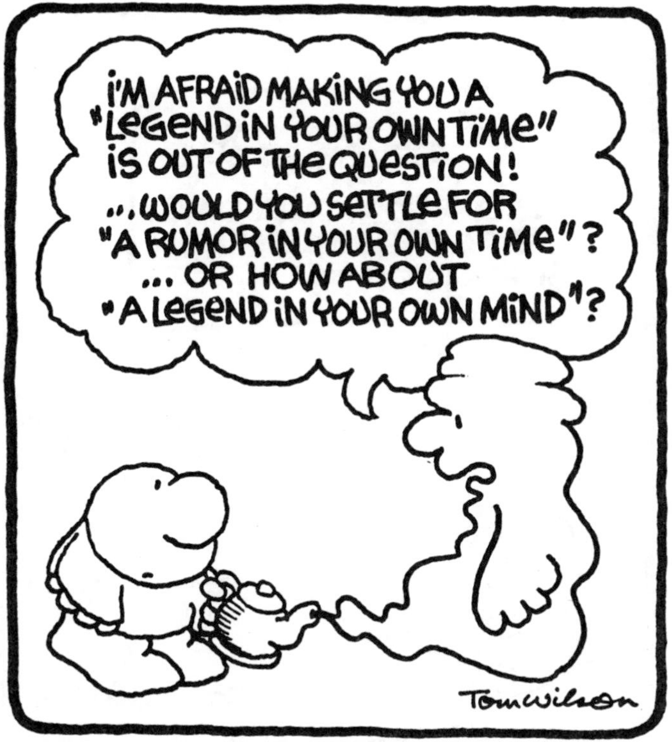
I'M AFRAID MAKING YOU A "LEGEND IN YOUR OWN TIME" IS OUT OF THE QUESTION! ...WOULD YOU SETTLE FOR "A RUMOR IN YOUR OWN TIME"? ... OR HOW ABOUT "A LEGEND IN YOUR OWN MIND"?
Tom Wilson

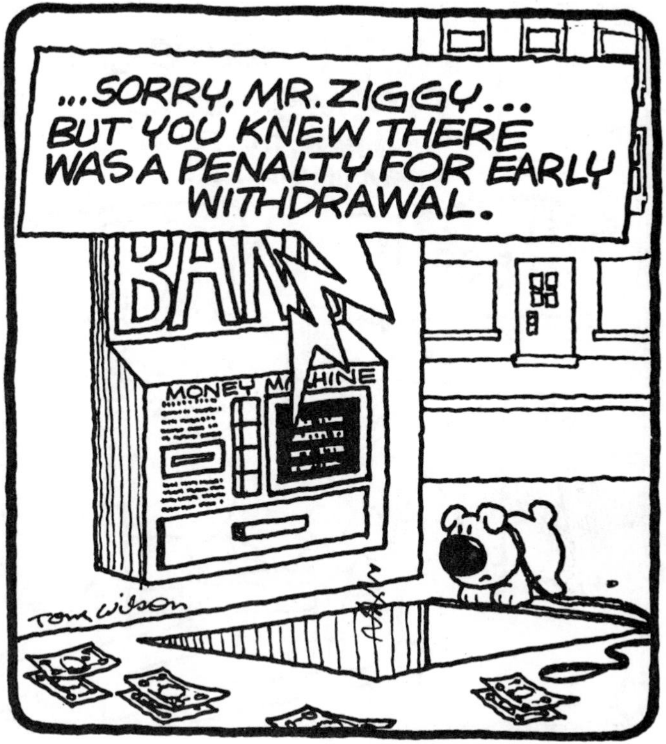
...SORRY, MR. ZIGGY... BUT YOU KNEW THERE WAS A PENALTY FOR EARLY WITHDRAWAL.
MONEY MACHINE
Tom Wilson

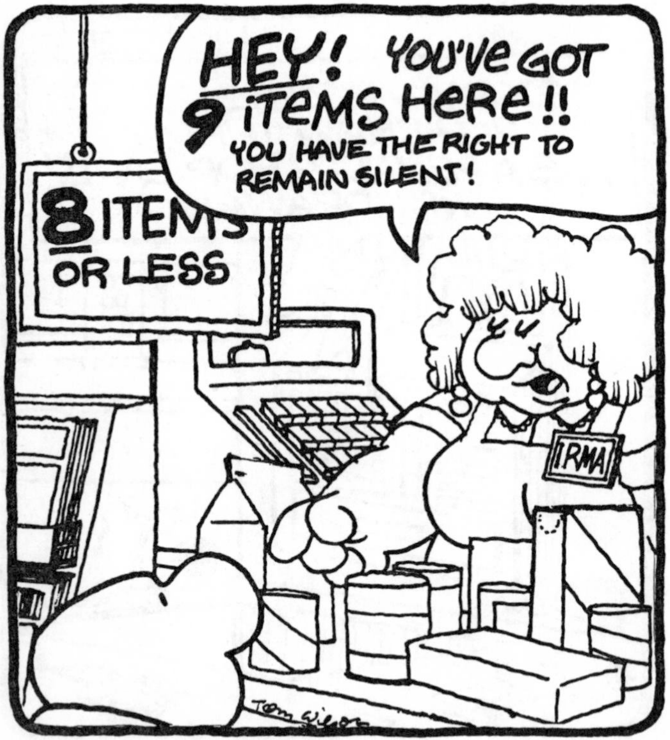
8 ITEMS OR LESS
HEY! YOU'VE GOT 9 ITEMS HERE!! YOU HAVE THE RIGHT TO REMAIN SILENT!
IRMA
Tom Wilson

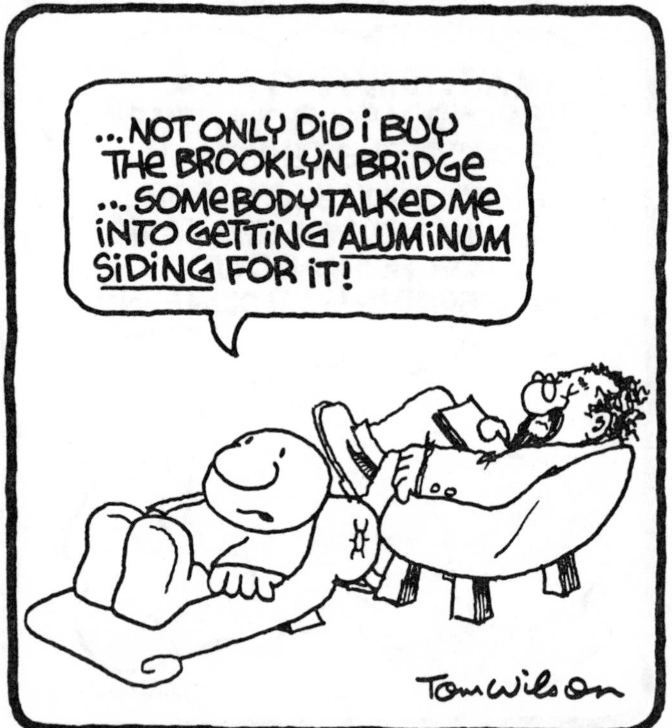
...NOT ONLY DID I BUY THE BROOKLYN BRIDGE ...SOMEBODY TALKED ME INTO GETTING ALUMINUM SIDING FOR IT!
Tom Wilson

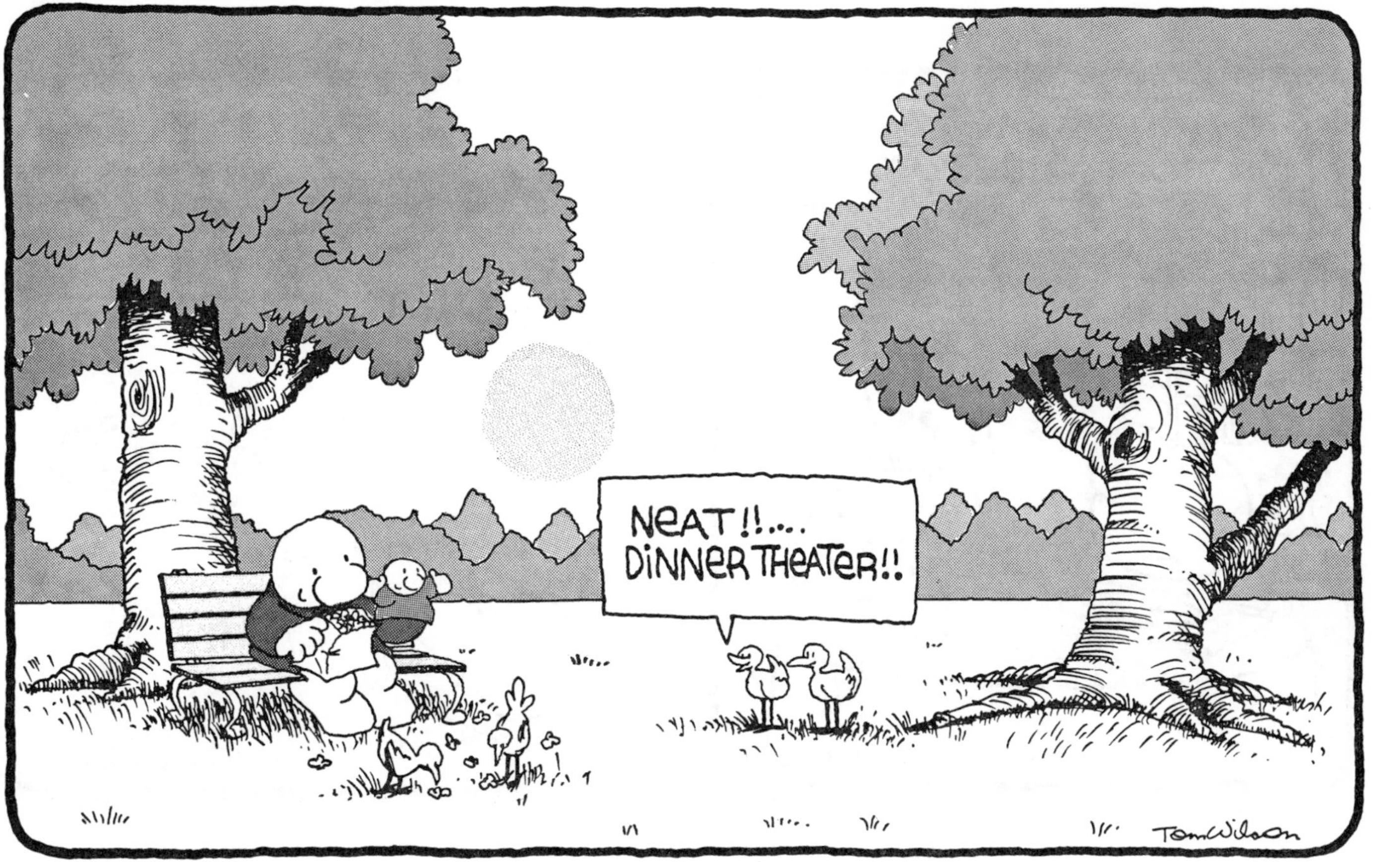
NEAT!!....
DINNER THEATER!!
TomWilson

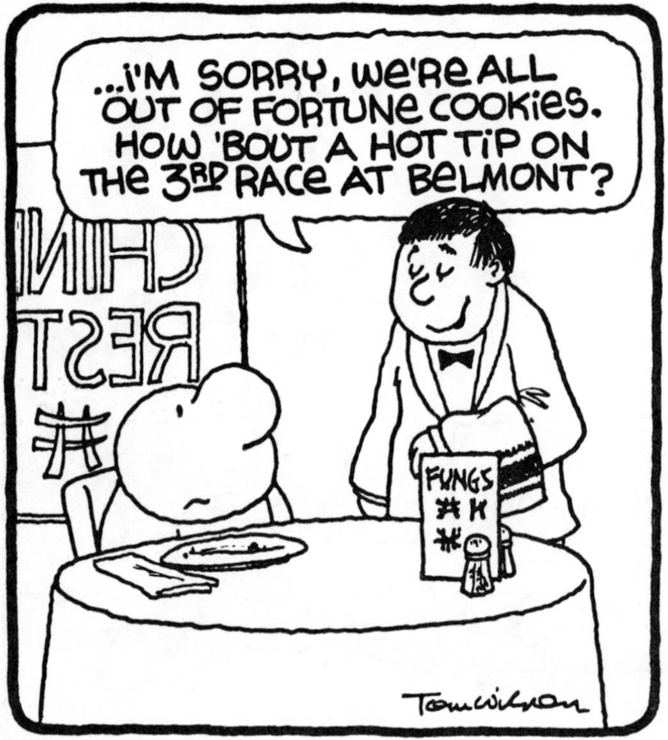
...I'M SORRY, WE'RE ALL OUT OF FORTUNE COOKIES. HOW 'BOUT A HOT TIP ON THE 3RD RACE AT BELMONT?
FUNGS
Tom Wilson

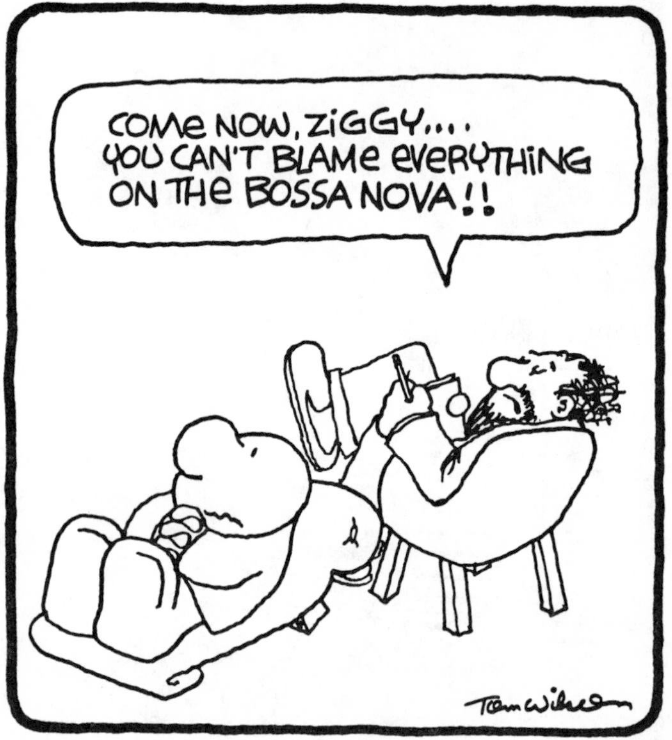
COME NOW, ZIGGY.... YOU CAN'T BLAME EVERYTHING ON THE BOSSA NOVA!!
Tom Wilson

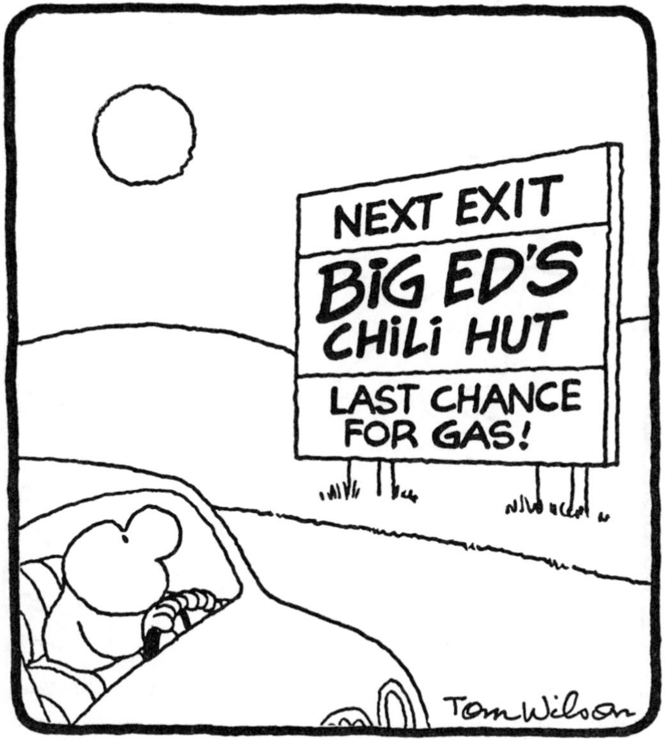
NEXT EXIT
BIG ED'S
CHILI HUT
LAST CHANCE
FOR GAS!
Tom Wilson

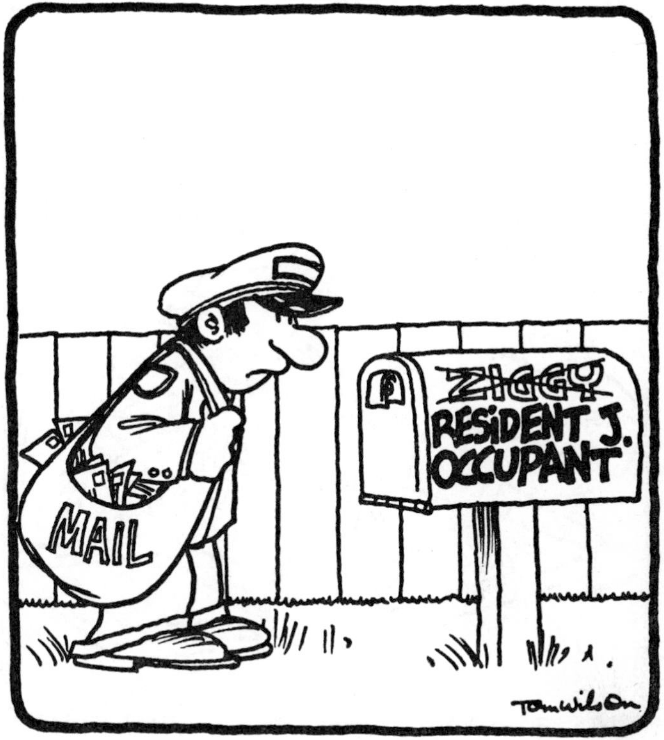
ZIGGY
RESIDENT J.
OCCUPANT
MAIL
Tom Wilson

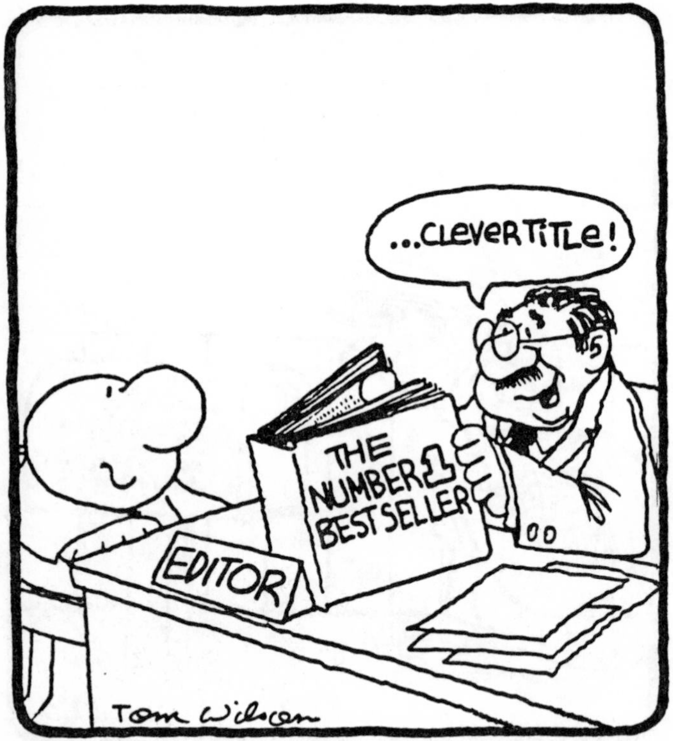
THE NUMBER 1 BEST SELLER
EDITOR
...CLEVER TITLE!
Tom Wilson

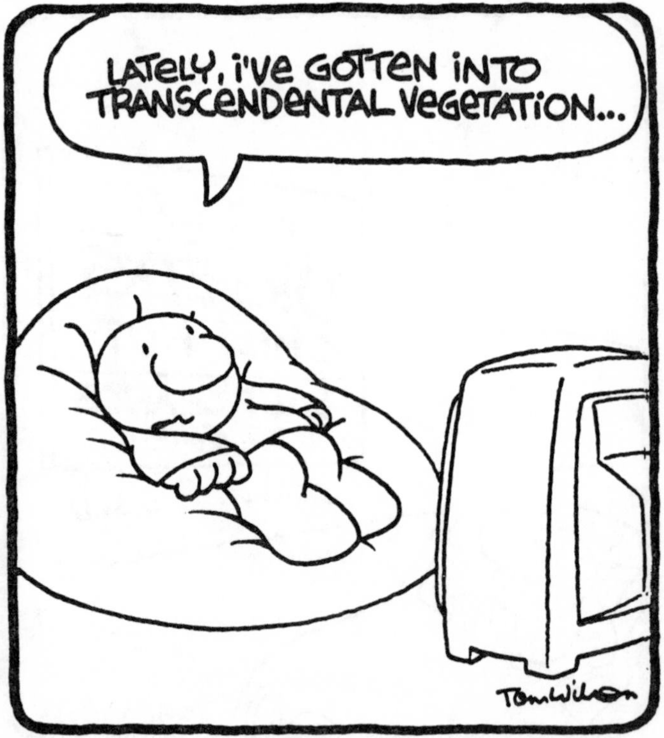
LATELY, I'VE GOTTEN INTO TRANSCENDENTAL VEGETATION...
Tom Wilson

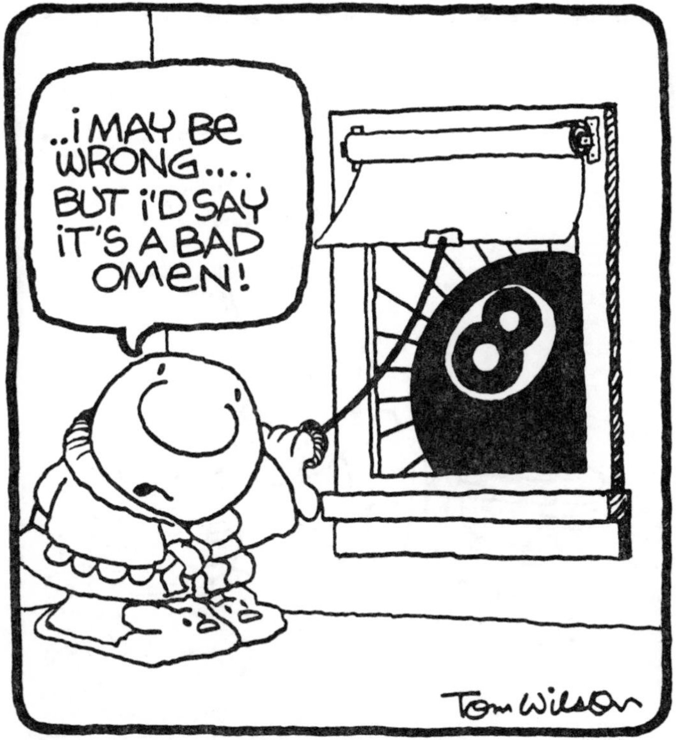
..i MAY BE WRONG.... BUT i'D SAY iT'S A BAD OMEN!
Tom Wilson

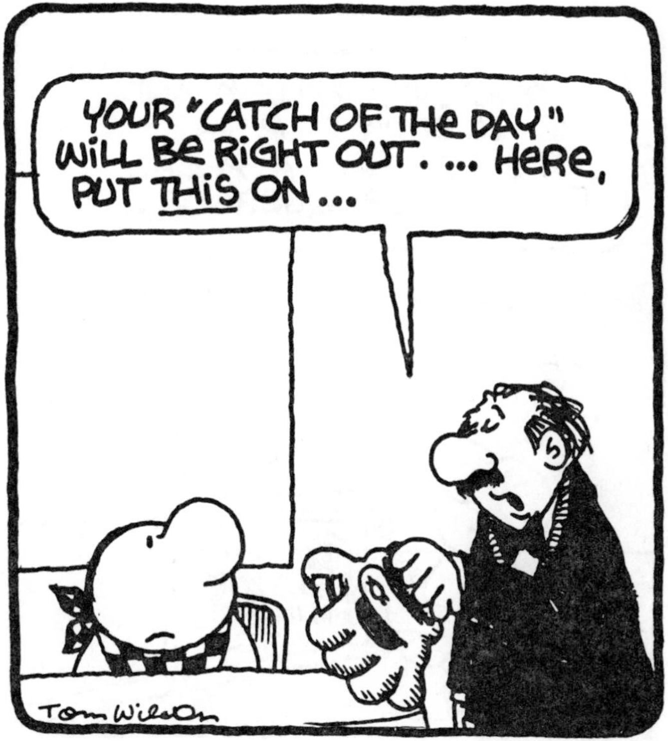
YOUR "CATCH OF THE DAY" WiLL BE RiGHT OUT. ... HERE, PUT THiS ON...
Tom Wilson

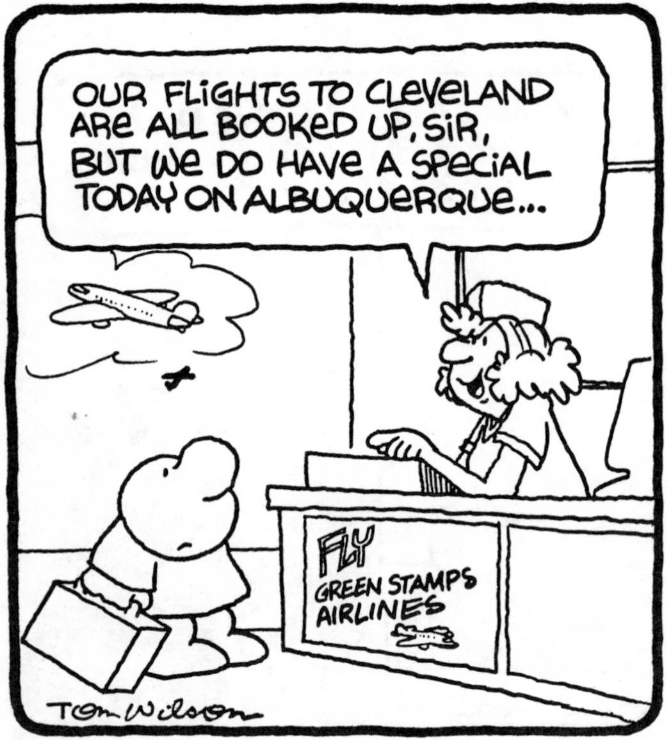
OUR FLIGHTS TO CLEVELAND ARE ALL BOOKED UP, SIR, BUT WE DO HAVE A SPECIAL TODAY ON ALBUQUERQUE...
FLY
GREEN STAMPS AIRLINES
TOM WILSON

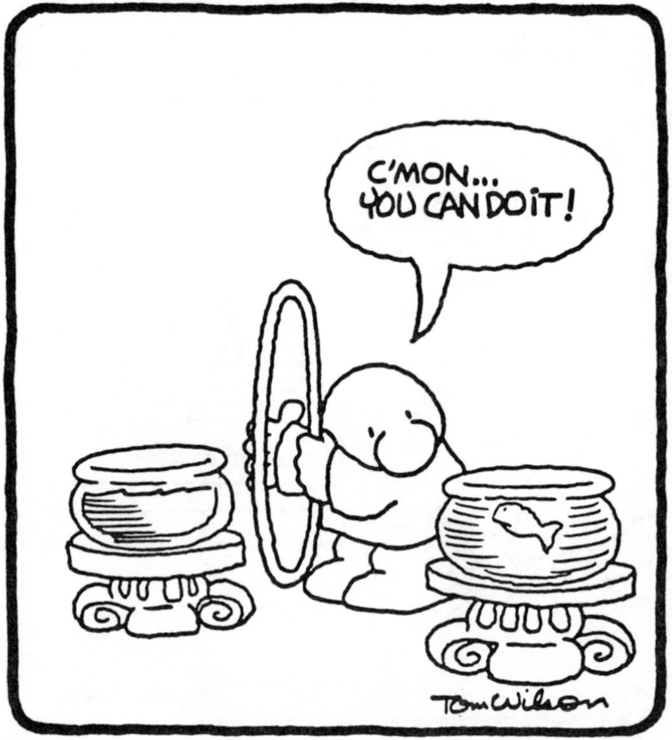
C'MON... YOU CAN DO IT!
TOM WILSON

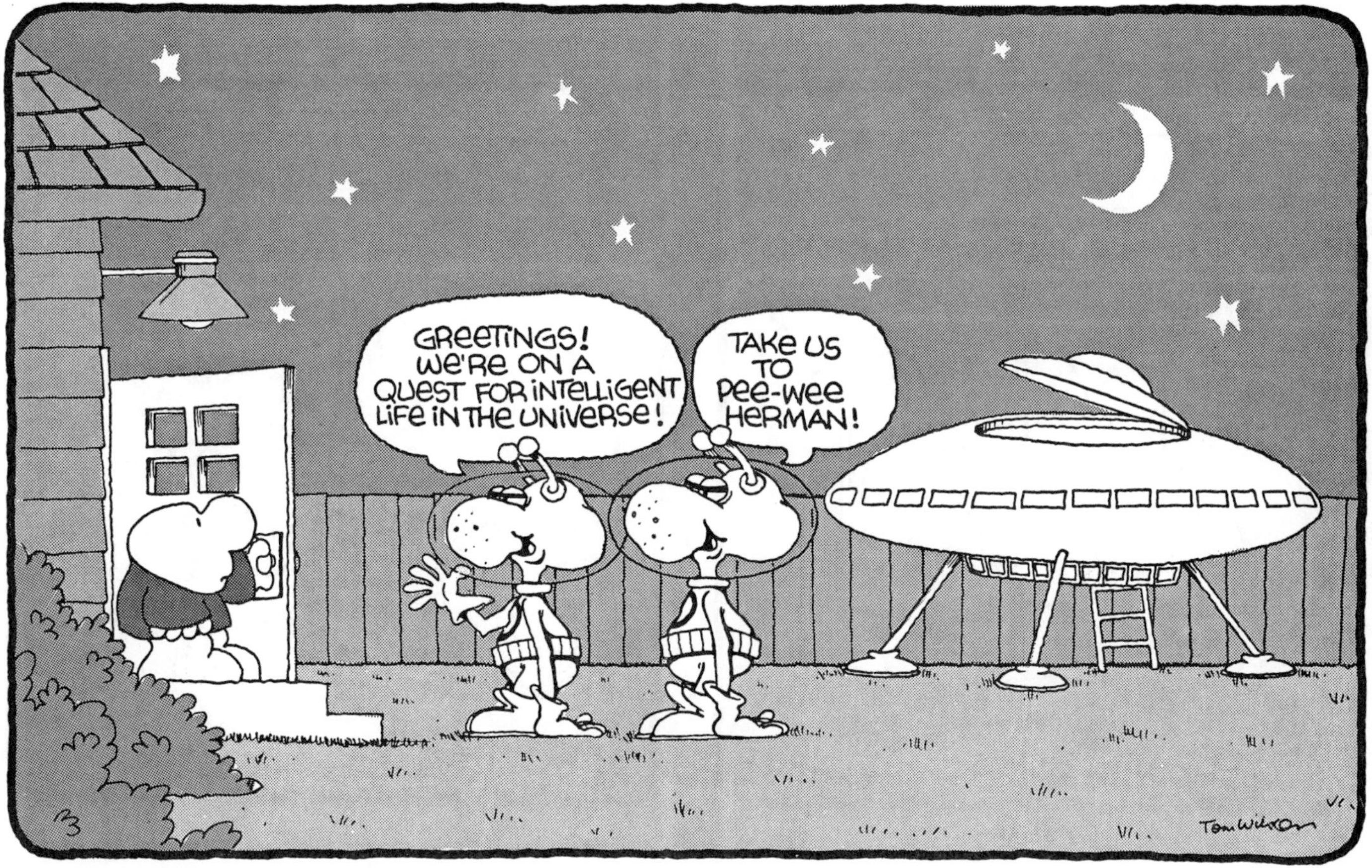
GREETINGS! WE'RE ON A QUEST FOR INTELLIGENT LIFE IN THE UNIVERSE!
TAKE US TO PEE-WEE HERMAN!
Tom Wilson

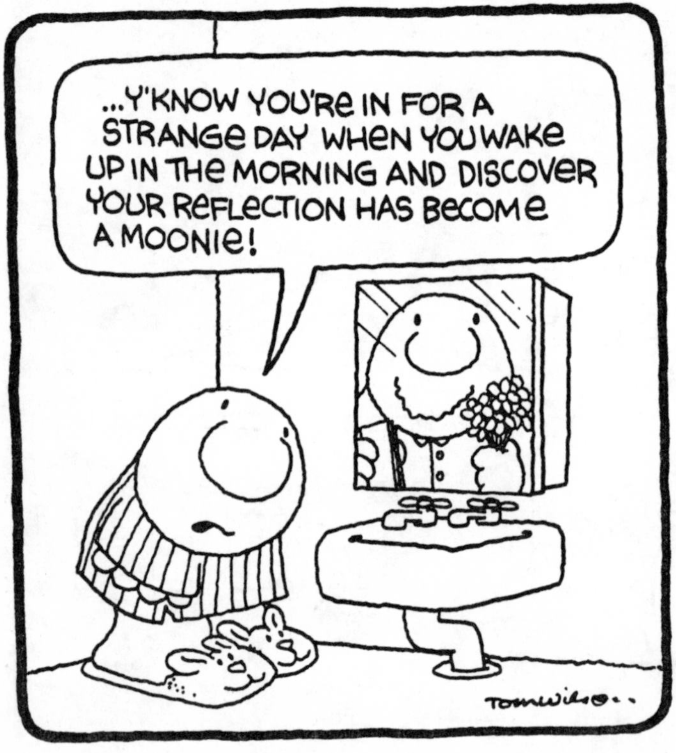
...Y'KNOW YOU'RE IN FOR A STRANGE DAY WHEN YOU WAKE UP IN THE MORNING AND DISCOVER YOUR REFLECTION HAS BECOME A MOONIE!
Tom Wilson

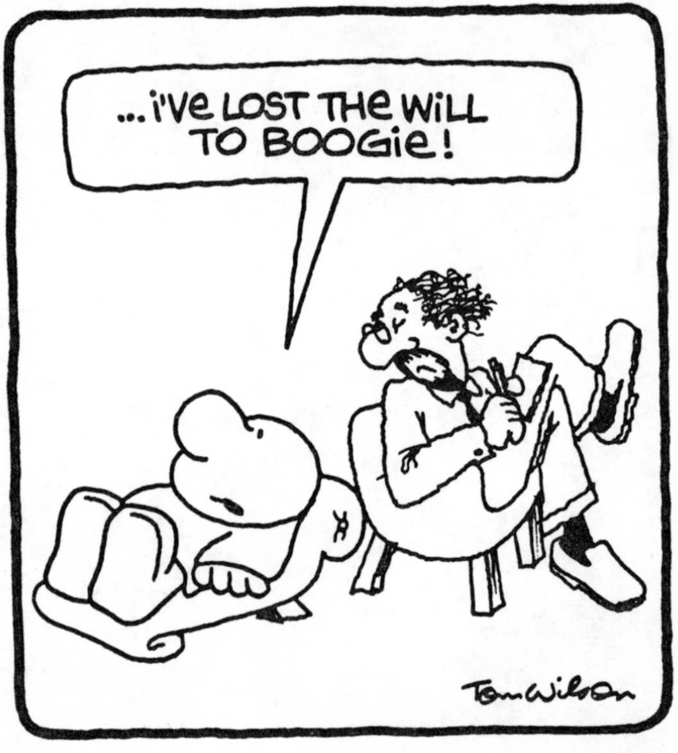
...I'VE LOST THE WILL TO BOOGIE!
Tom Wilson

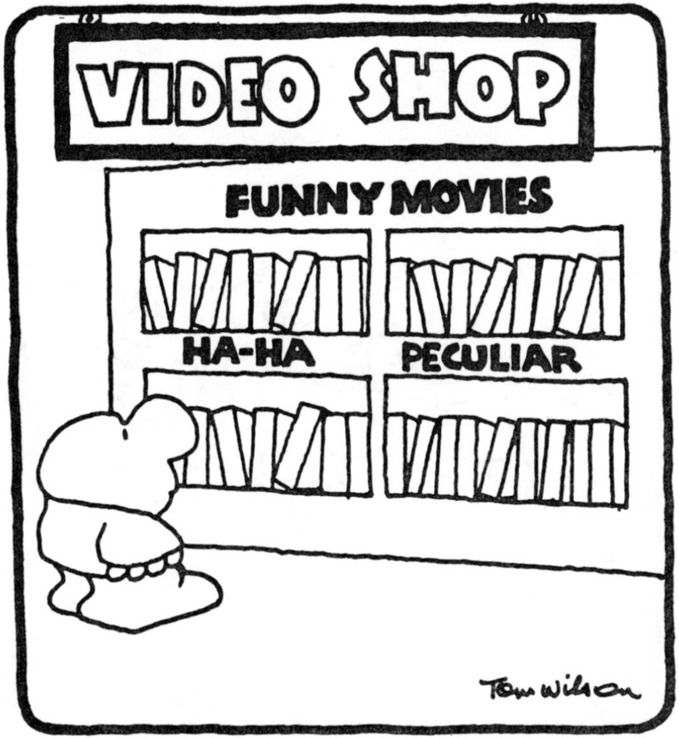
VIDEO SHOP
FUNNY MOVIES
HA-HA
PECULIAR
Tom Wilson

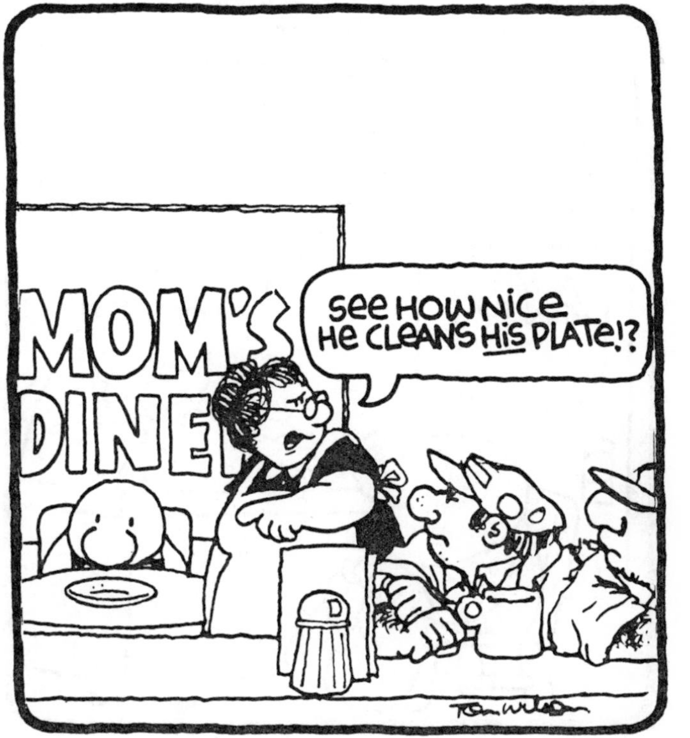
MOM'S
DINE
SEE HOW NICE HE CLEANS HIS PLATE!?
Tom Wilson

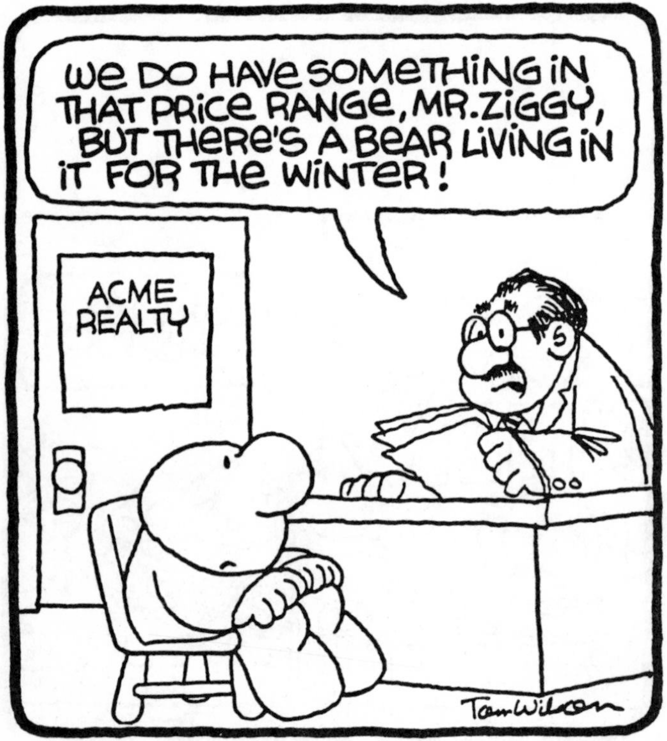
WE DO HAVE SOMETHING IN THAT PRICE RANGE, MR. ZIGGY, BUT THERE'S A BEAR LIVING IN IT FOR THE WINTER!
ACME REALTY
Tom Wilson

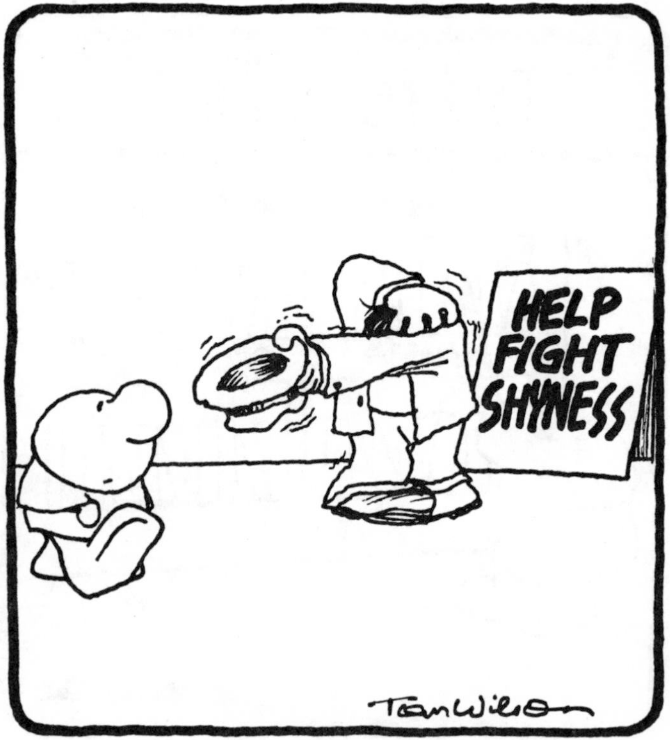
HELP FIGHT SHYNESS
Tom Wilson

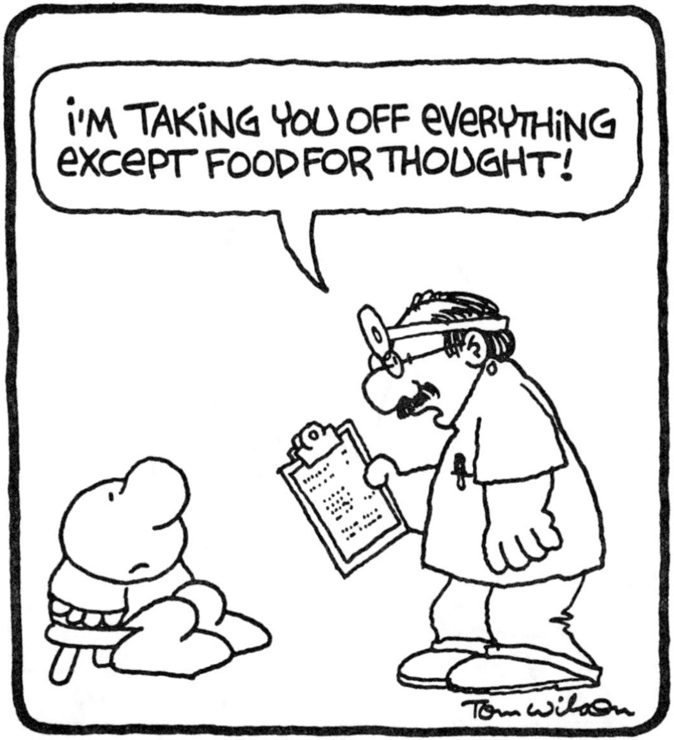
I'M TAKING YOU OFF EVERYTHING EXCEPT FOOD FOR THOUGHT!
Tom Wilson

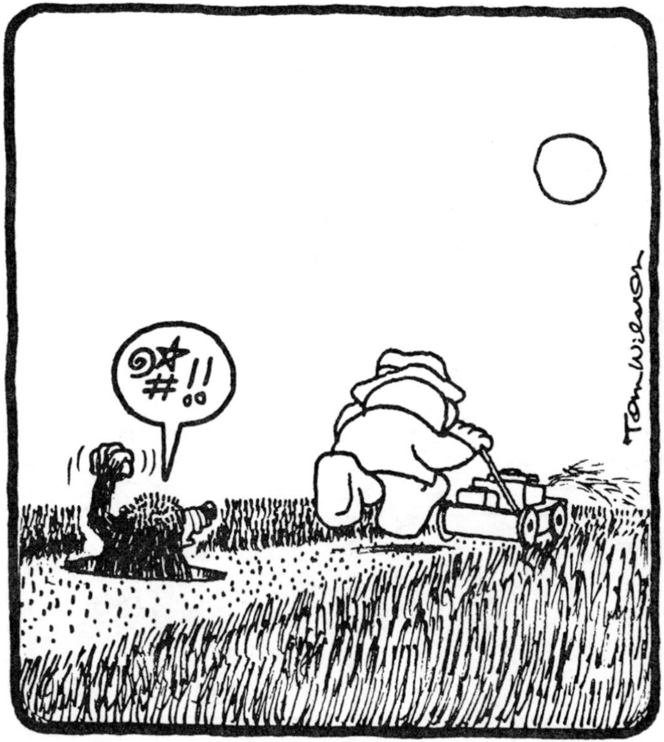
Tom Wilson

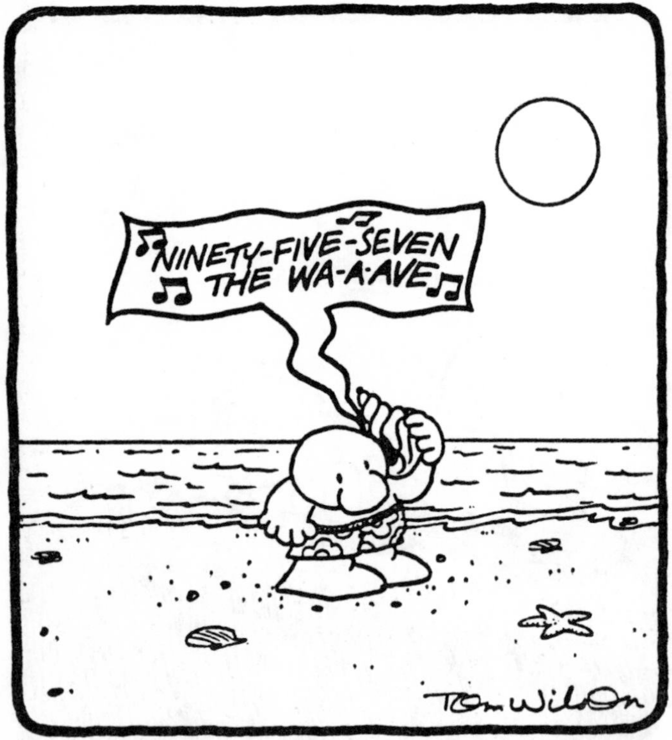
NINETY-FIVE-SEVEN
THE WA-A-AVE
TOM WILSON

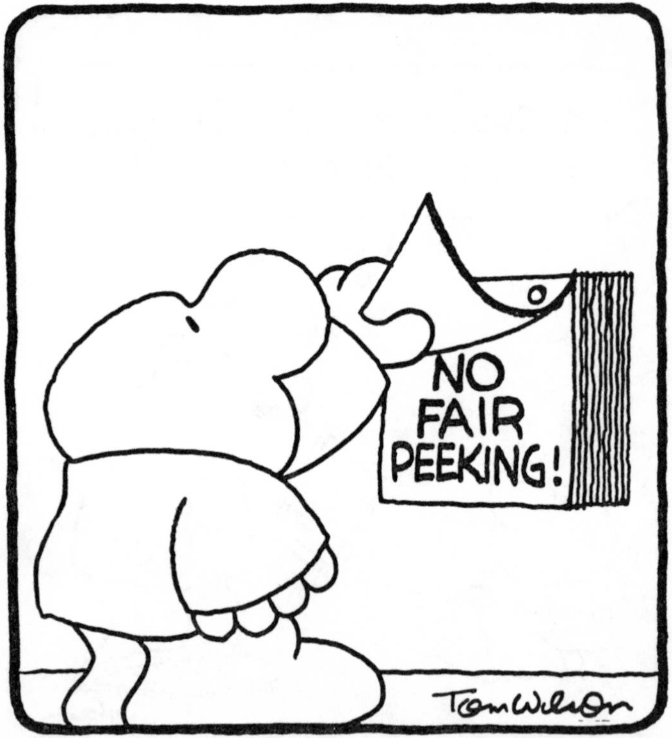
NO
FAIR
PEEKING!
TOM WILSON

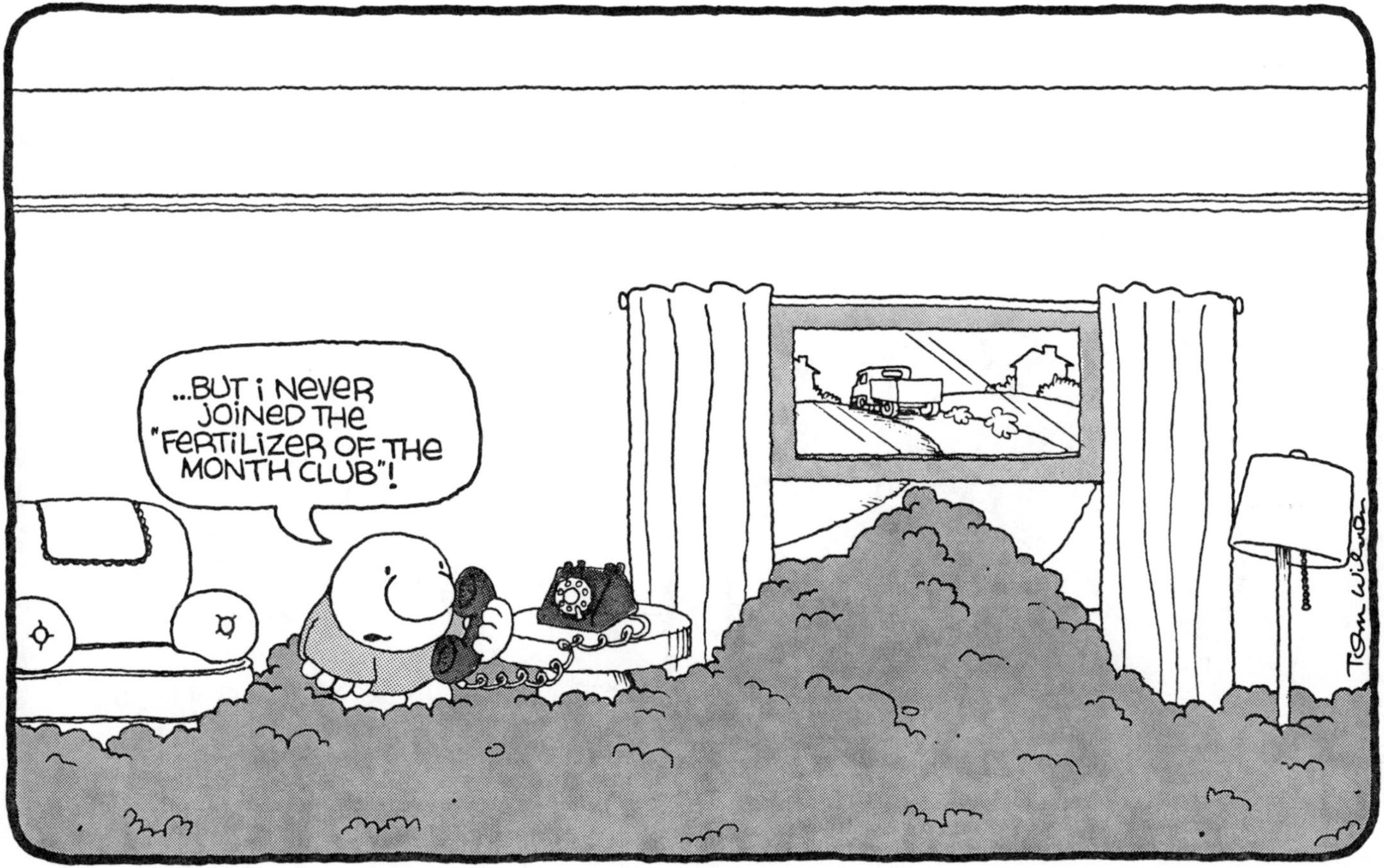
...BUT i NEVER JOINED THE "FERTILIZER OF THE MONTH CLUB"!
Tom Wilson

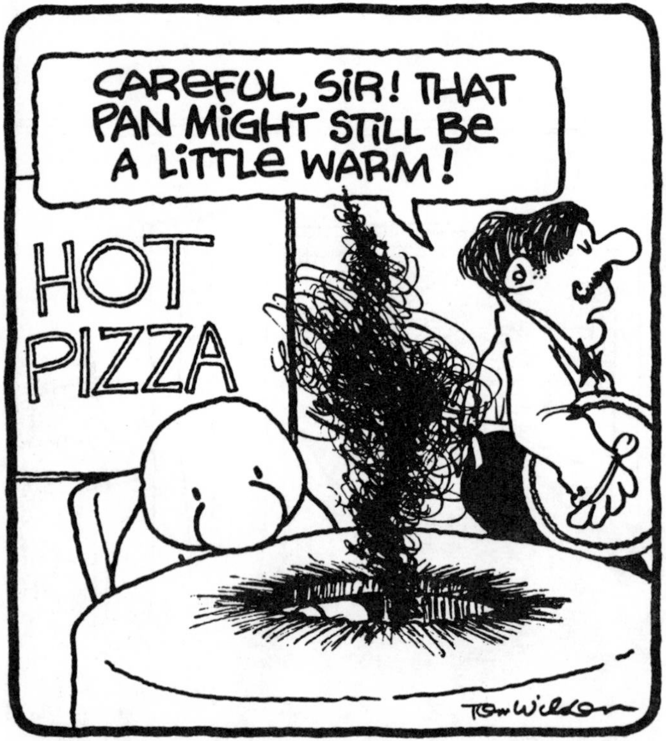
CAREFUL, SIR! THAT PAN MIGHT STILL BE A LITTLE WARM!
HOT PIZZA
TOM WILSON

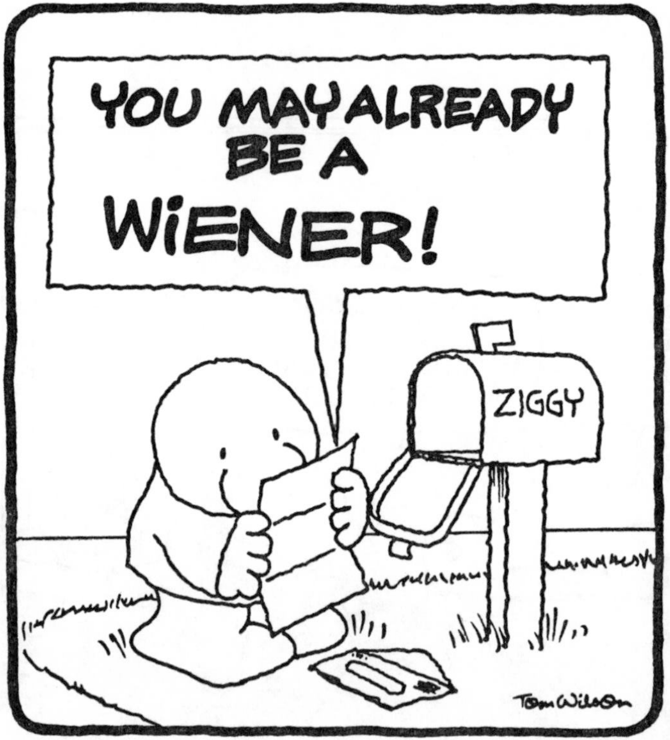
YOU MAY ALREADY BE A WIENER!
ZIGGY
TOM WILSON

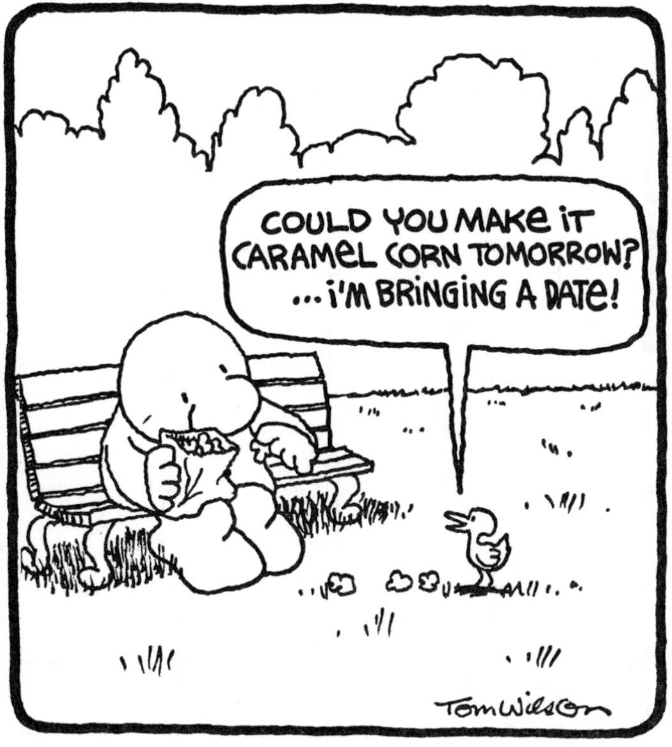
COULD YOU MAKE IT CARAMEL CORN TOMORROW? ...I'M BRINGING A DATE!
Tom Wilson

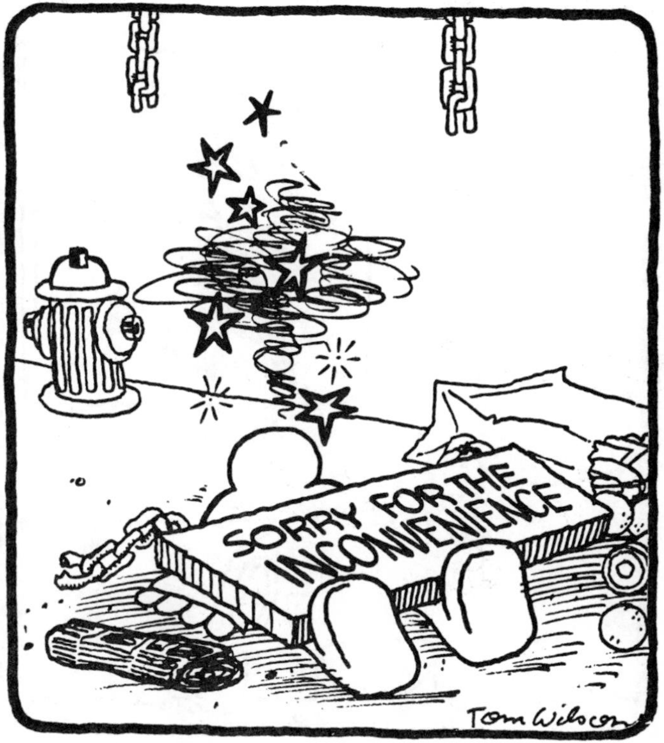
SORRY FOR THE INCONVENIENCE
Tom Wilson

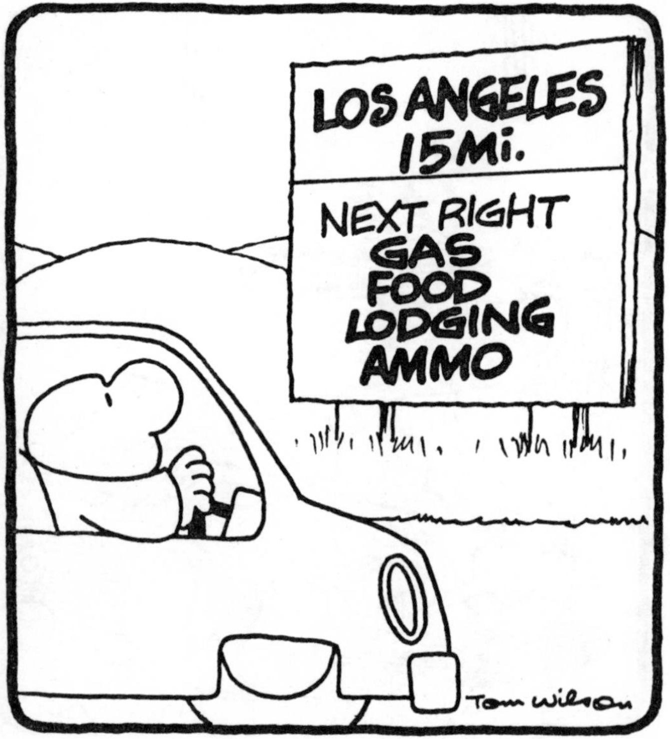
LOS ANGELES
15 Mi.
NEXT RIGHT
GAS
FOOD
LODGING
AMMO
Tom Wilson

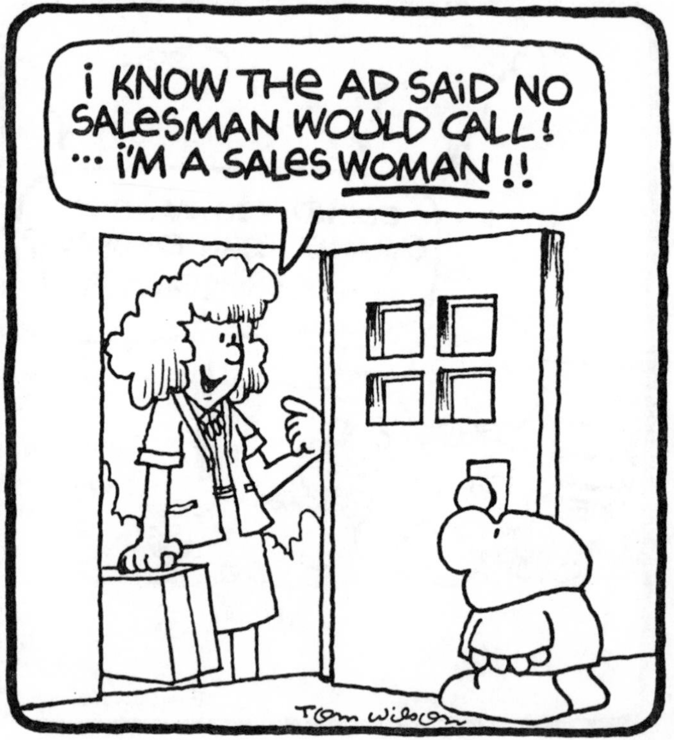
i KNOW THE AD SAiD NO SALESMAN WOULD CALL! ... i'M A SALES WOMAN !!
Tom Wilson

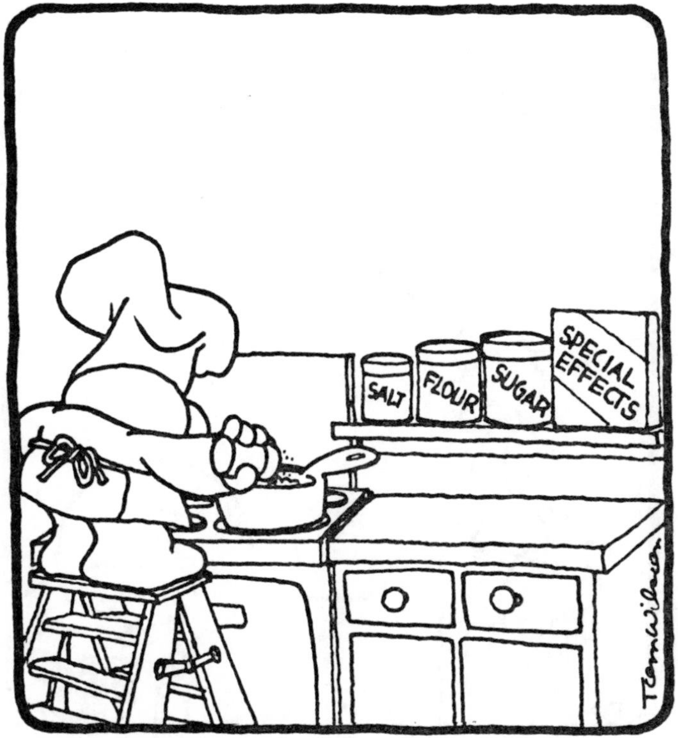
SALT
FLOUR
SUGAR
SPECIAL EFFECTS
TomWilson

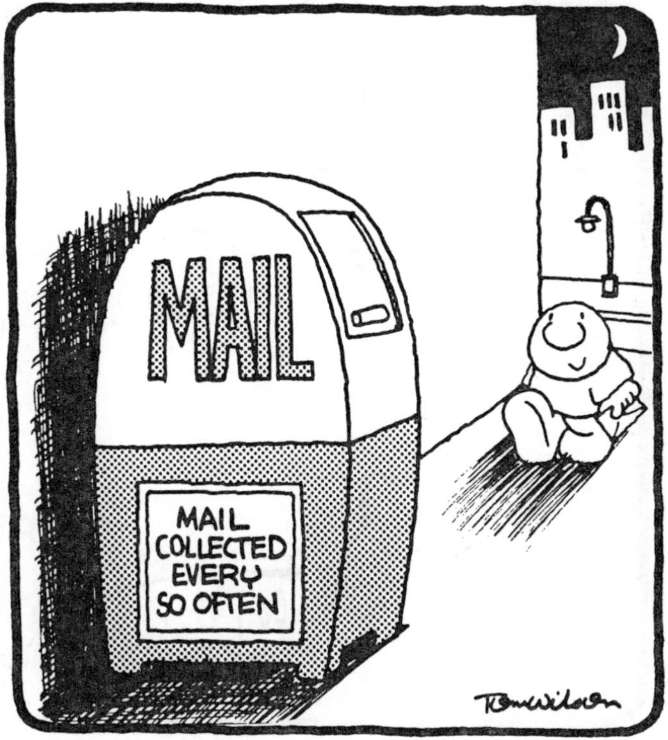
MAIL
MAIL COLLECTED EVERY SO OFTEN
TomWilson

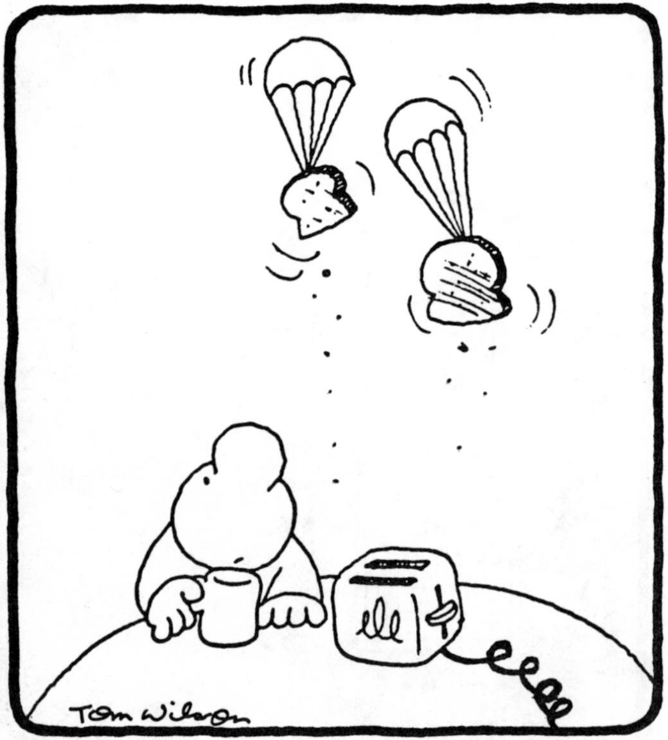

Tom Wilson

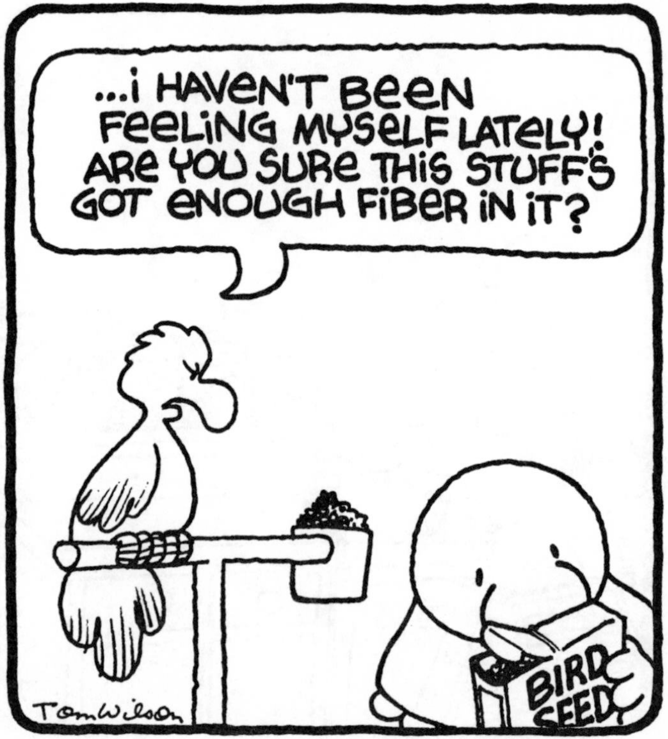

...i HAVEN'T BeeN FeeLiNG MYSeLF LATeLY! ARe YOU SURe THiS STUFF'S GOT eNOUGH FiBeR iN iT?
BIRD SEED
Tom Wilson

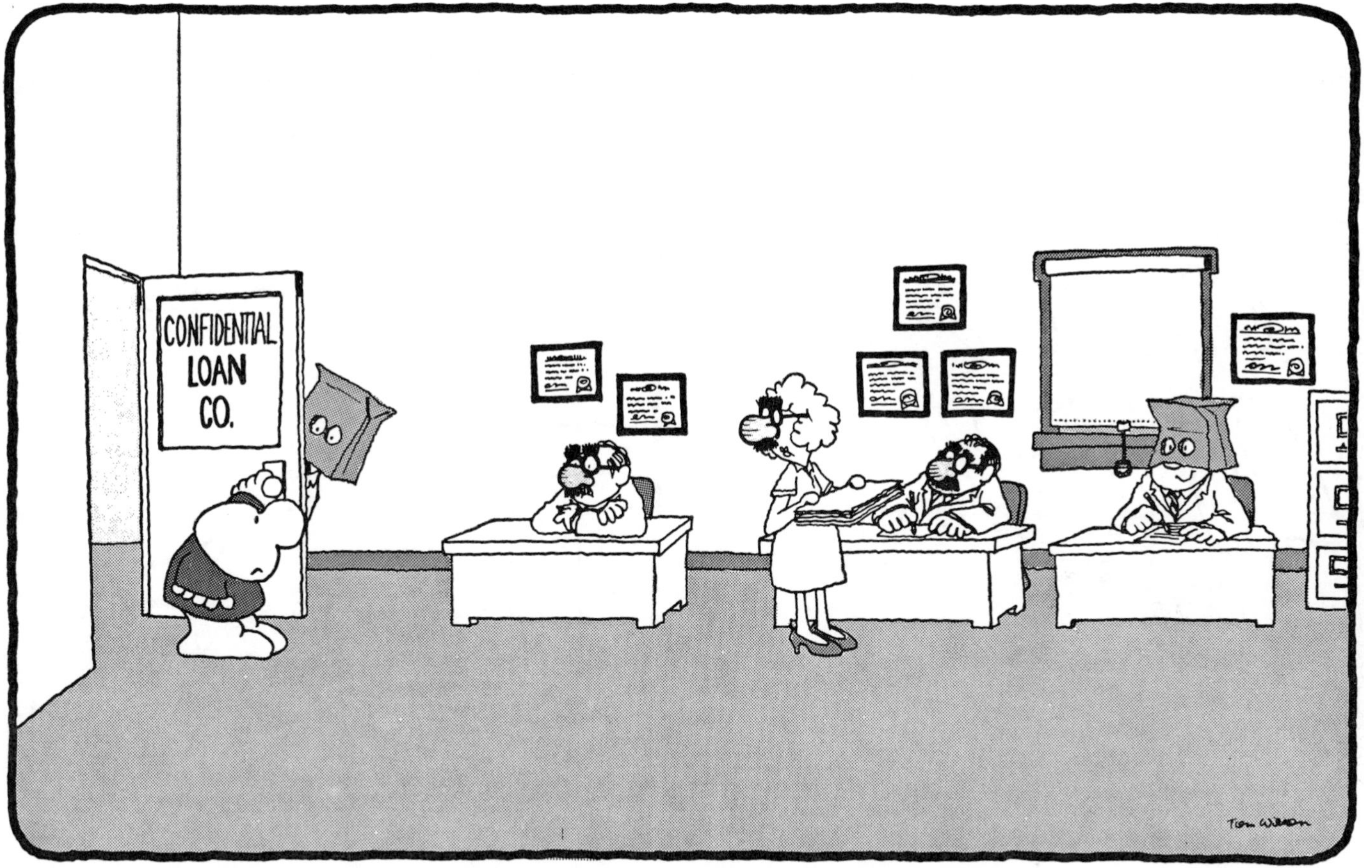
CONFIDENTIAL
LOAN
CO.

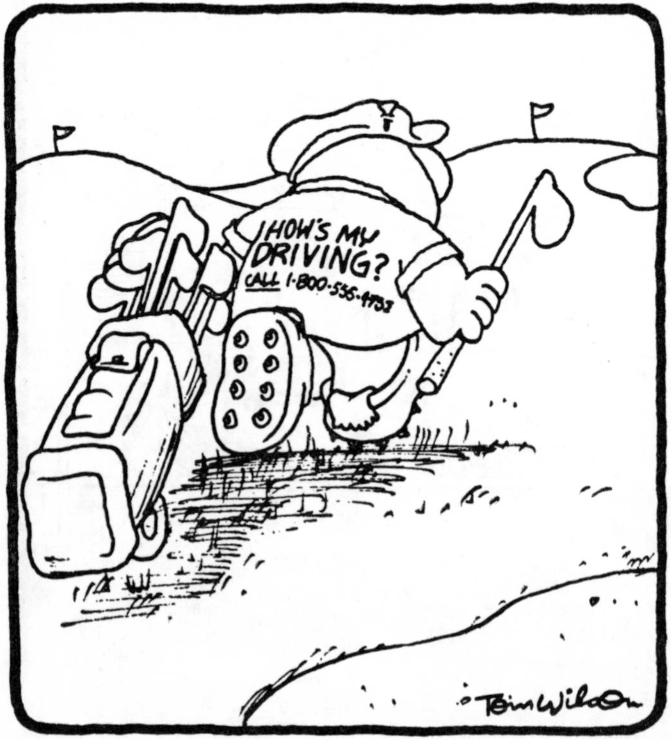
HOW'S MY DRIVING?
CALL 1-800-555
TOM WILSON

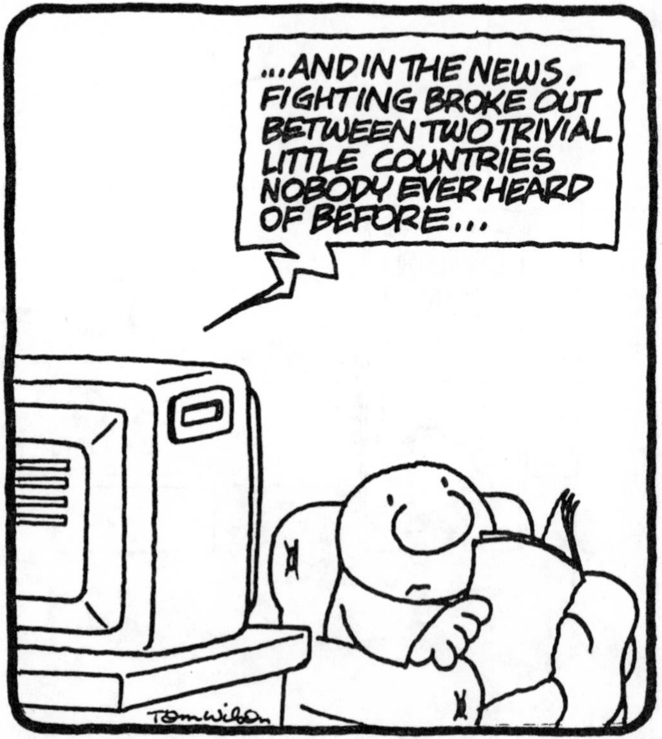
...AND IN THE NEWS, FIGHTING BROKE OUT BETWEEN TWO TRIVIAL LITTLE COUNTRIES NOBODY EVER HEARD OF BEFORE...
TOM WILSON

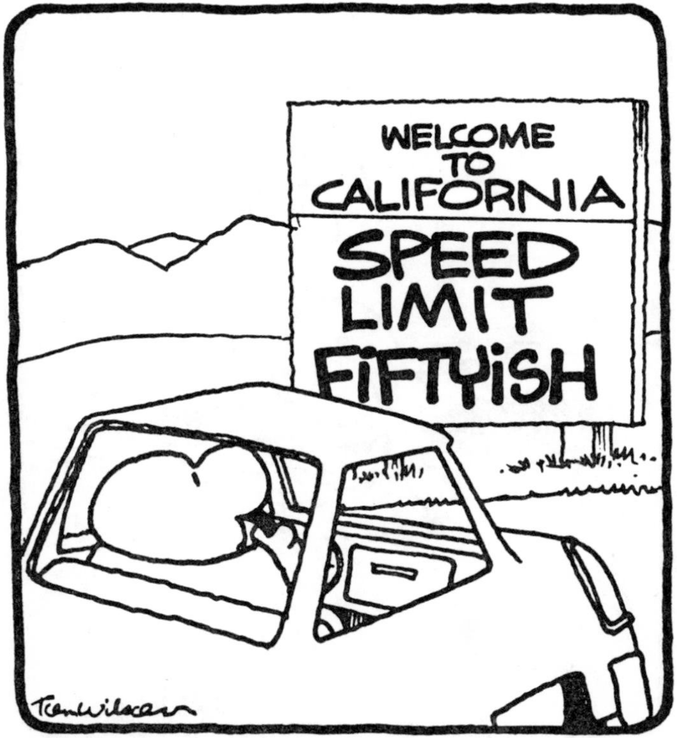
WELCOME TO CALIFORNIA
SPEED LIMIT FIFTYISH
Tom Wilson

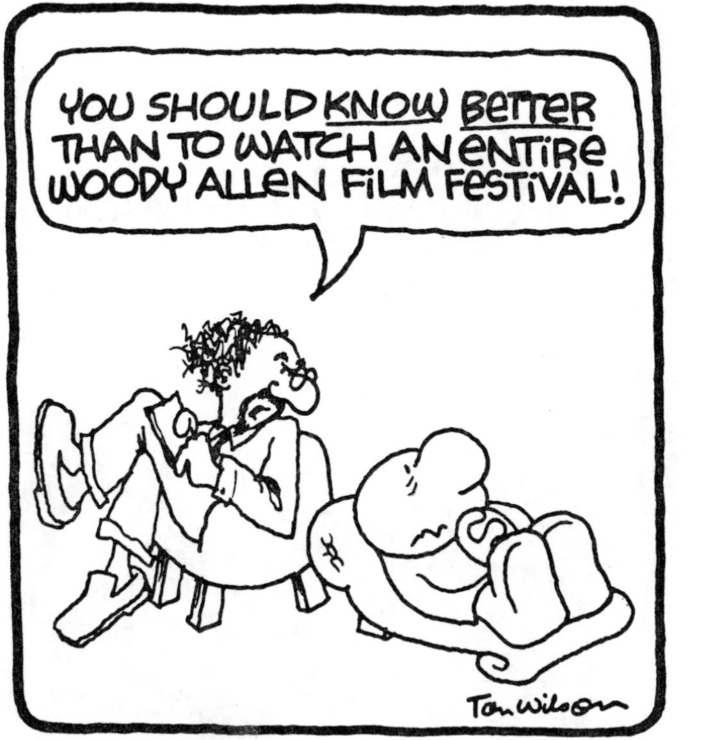
YOU SHOULD KNOW BETTER THAN TO WATCH AN ENTIRE WOODY ALLEN FILM FESTIVAL!
Tom Wilson

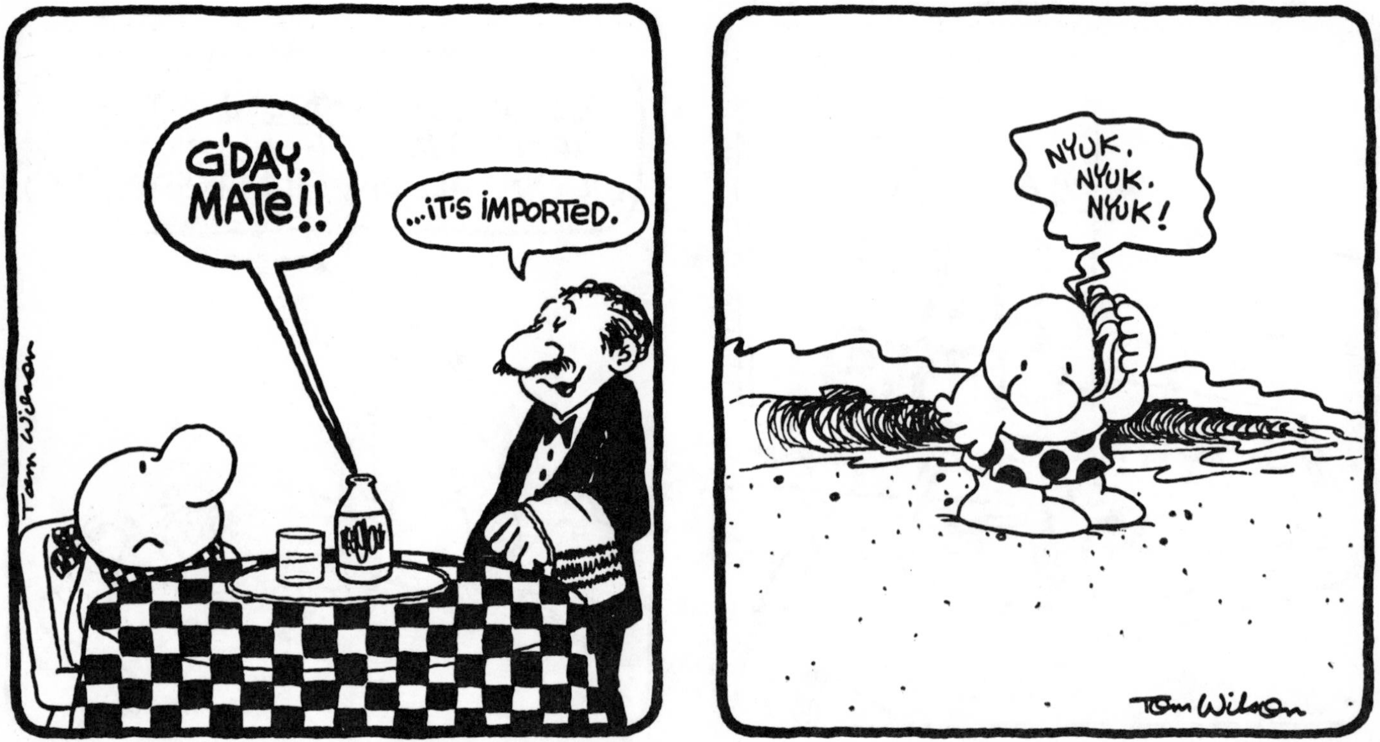
G'DAY, MATE!!
...IT'S IMPORTED.
Tom Wilson
NYUK. NYUK. NYUK!
TOM WILSON

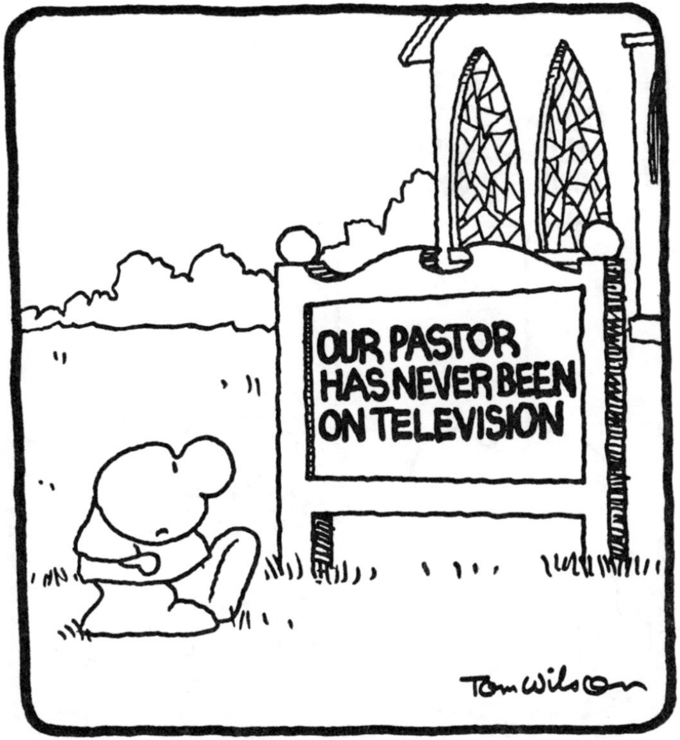
OUR PASTOR HAS NEVER BEEN ON TELEVISION
Tom Wilson

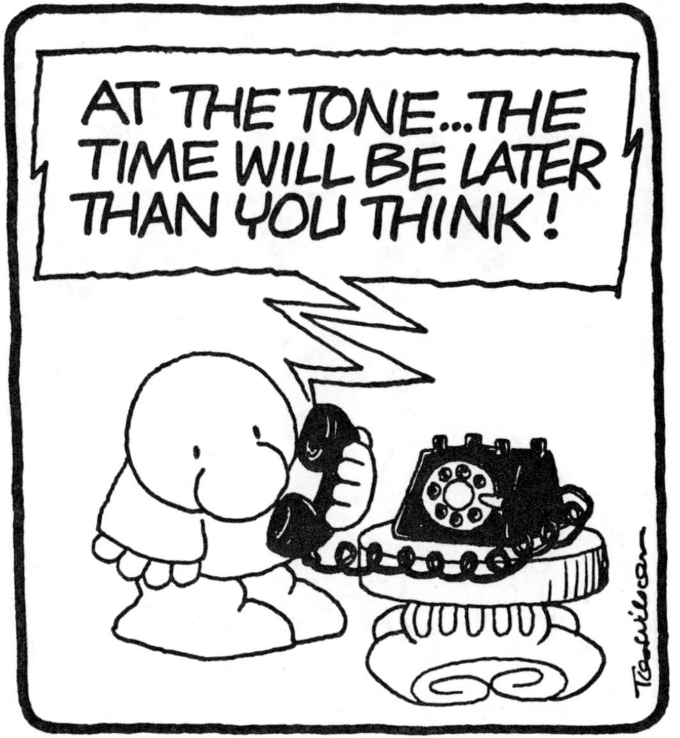
AT THE TONE...THE TIME WILL BE LATER THAN YOU THINK!
Tom Wilson

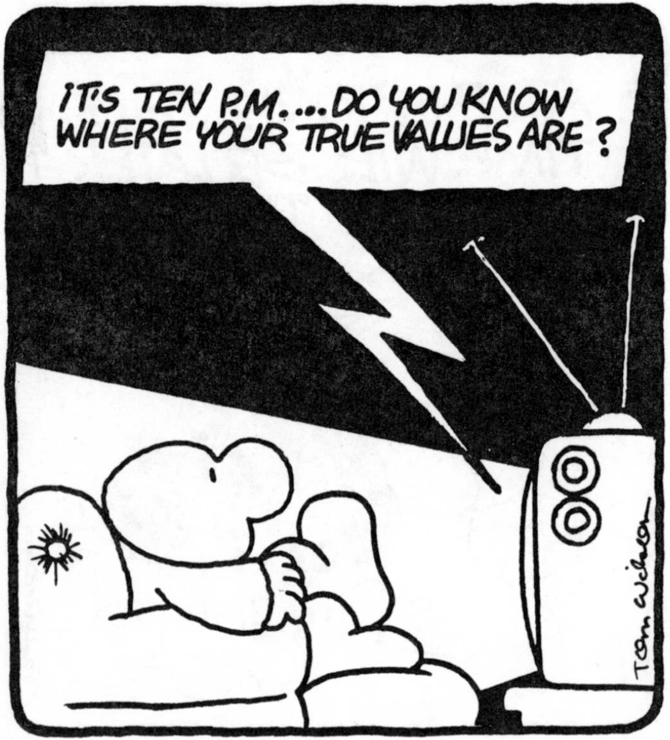
IT'S TEN P.M.... DO YOU KNOW WHERE YOUR TRUE VALUES ARE ?
Tom Wilson

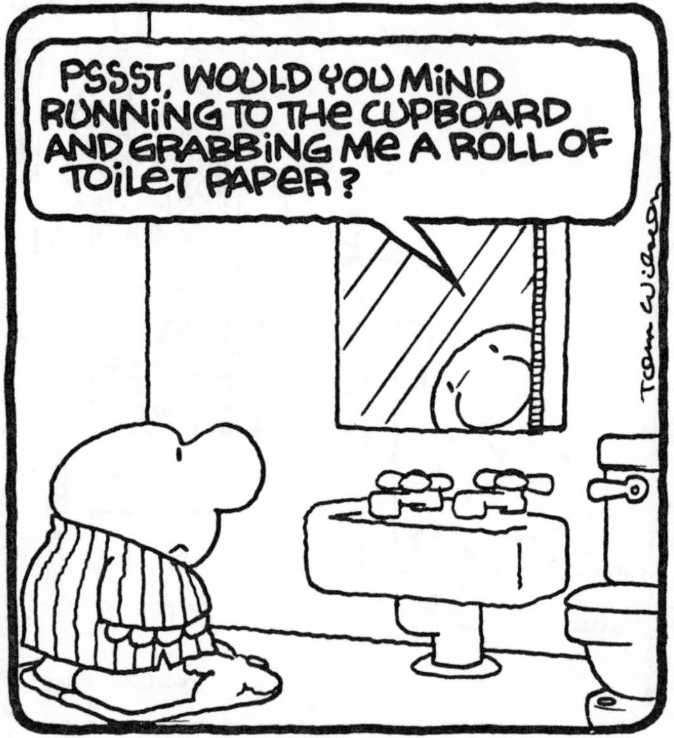
PSSST, WOULD YOU MIND RUNNING TO THE CUPBOARD AND GRABBING ME A ROLL OF TOILET PAPER ?
Tom Wilson

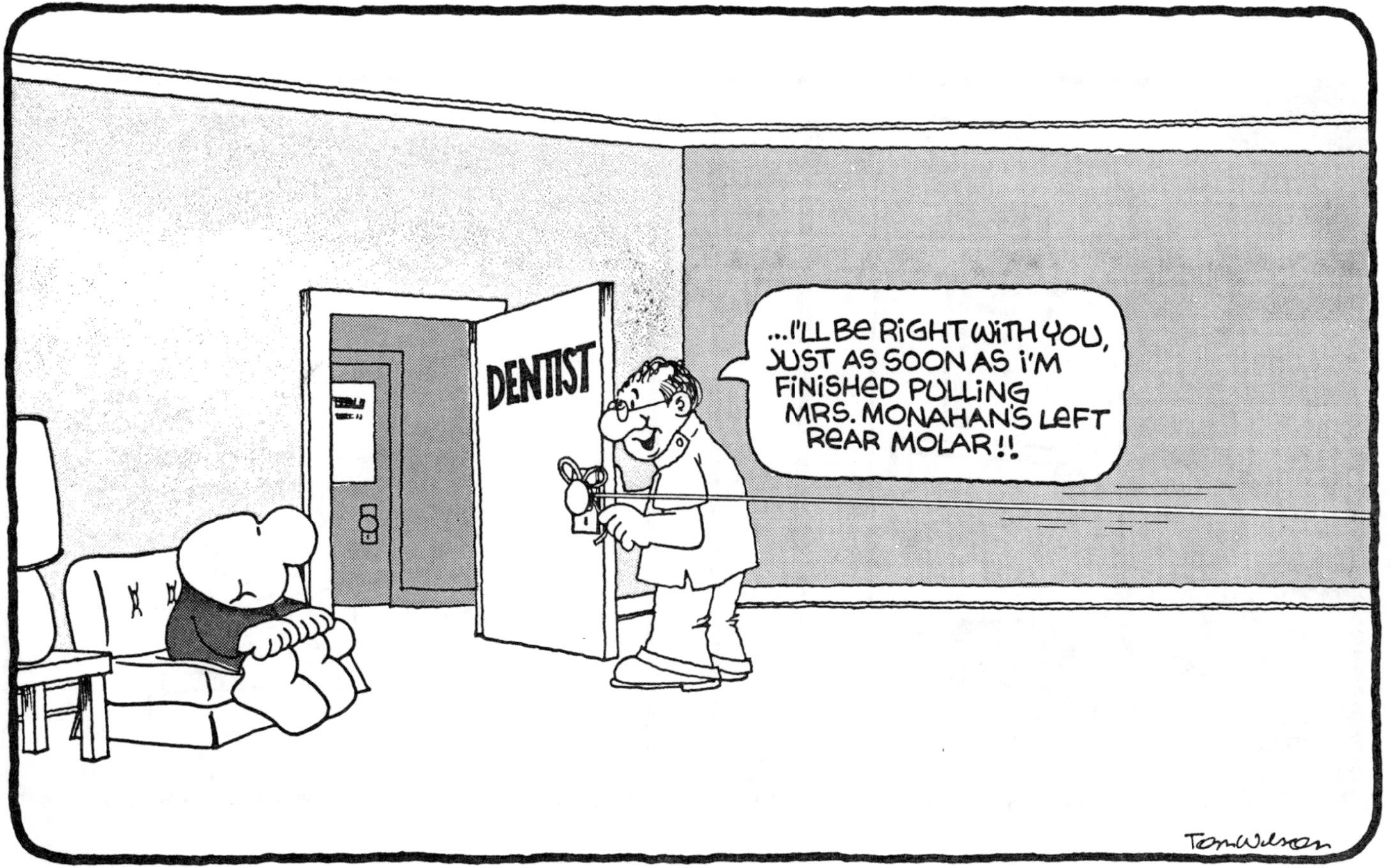
DENTIST
...I'LL BE RIGHT WITH YOU, JUST AS SOON AS I'M FINISHED PULLING MRS. MONAHAN'S LEFT REAR MOLAR!!
Tom Wilson

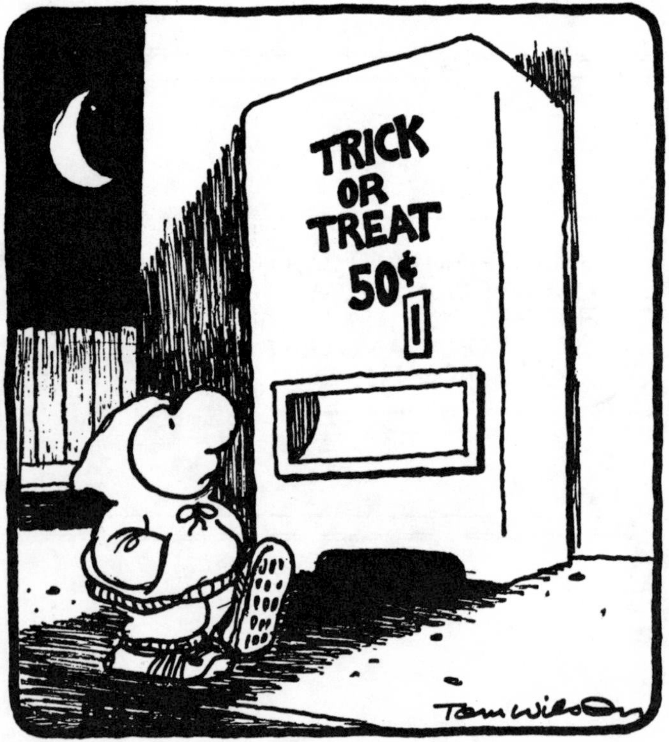

TRICK OR TREAT 50¢
Tom Wilson

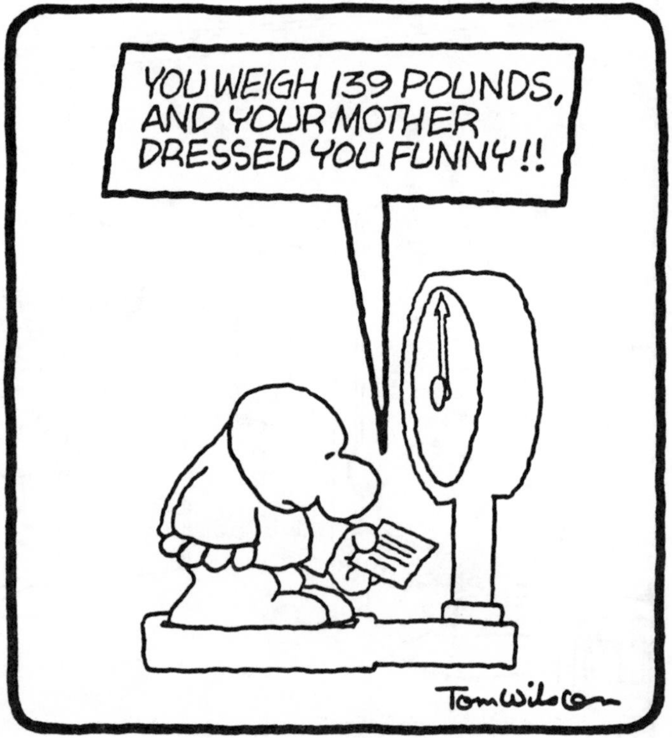

YOU WEIGH 139 POUNDS, AND YOUR MOTHER DRESSED YOU FUNNY!!
Tom Wilson

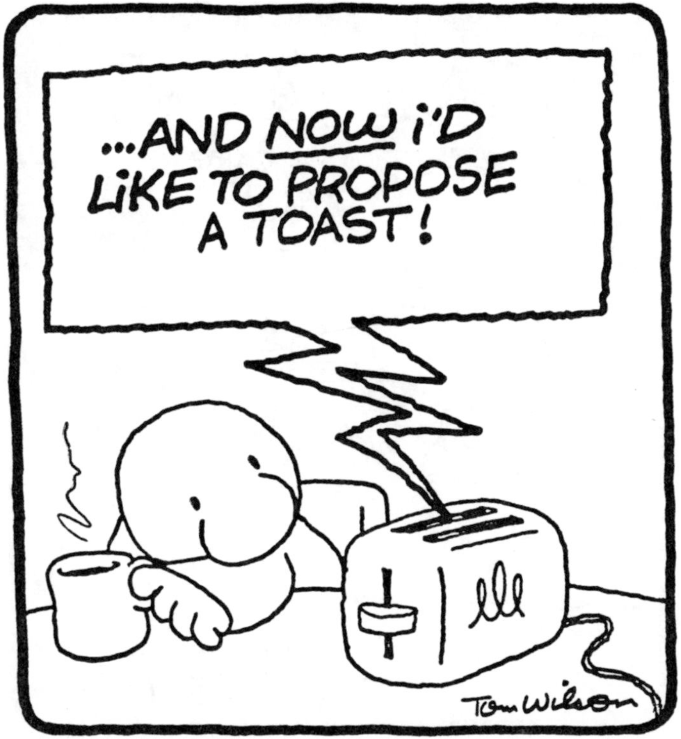
...AND NOW i'D LiKE TO PROPOSE A TOAST!
Tom Wilson

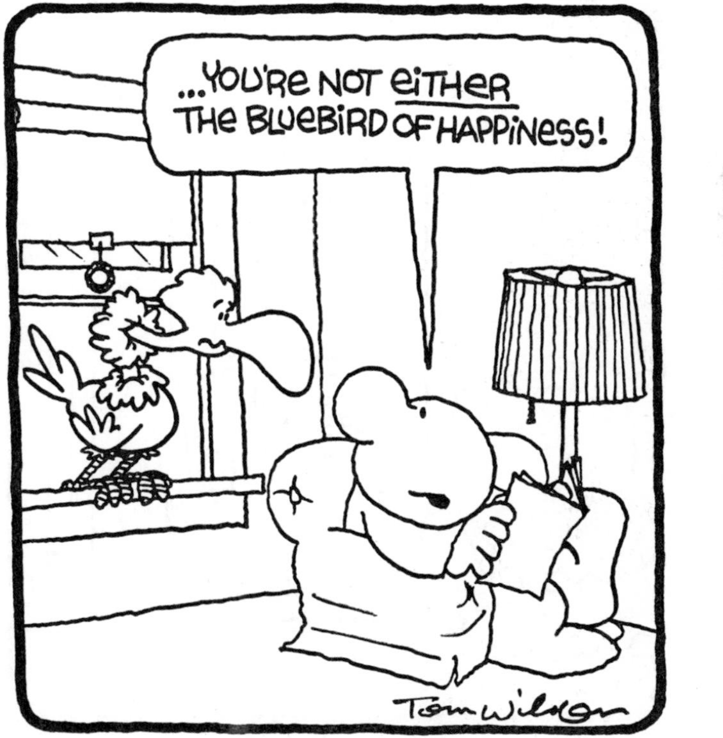
...YOU'RE NOT EiTHER THE BLUEBiRD OF HAPPiNESS!
Tom Wilson

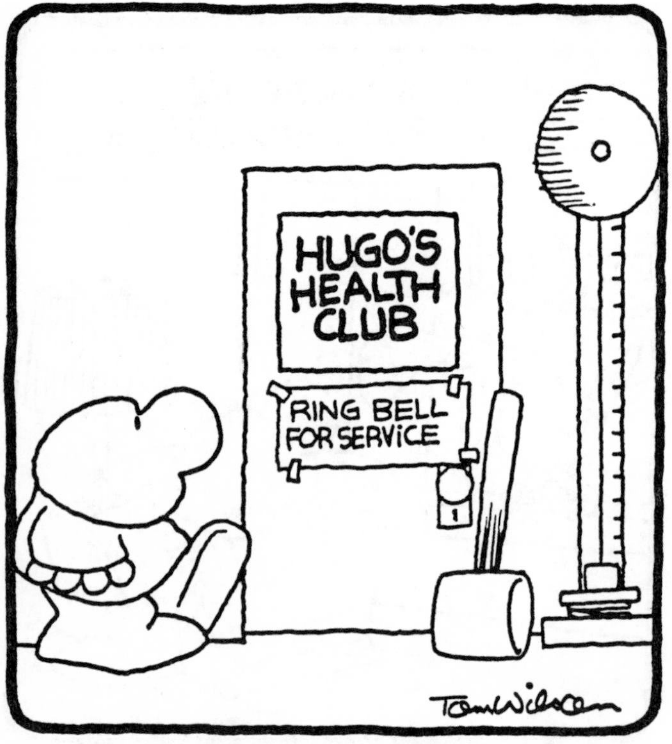
HUGO'S HEALTH CLUB
RING BELL FOR SERVICE
1
Tom Wilson

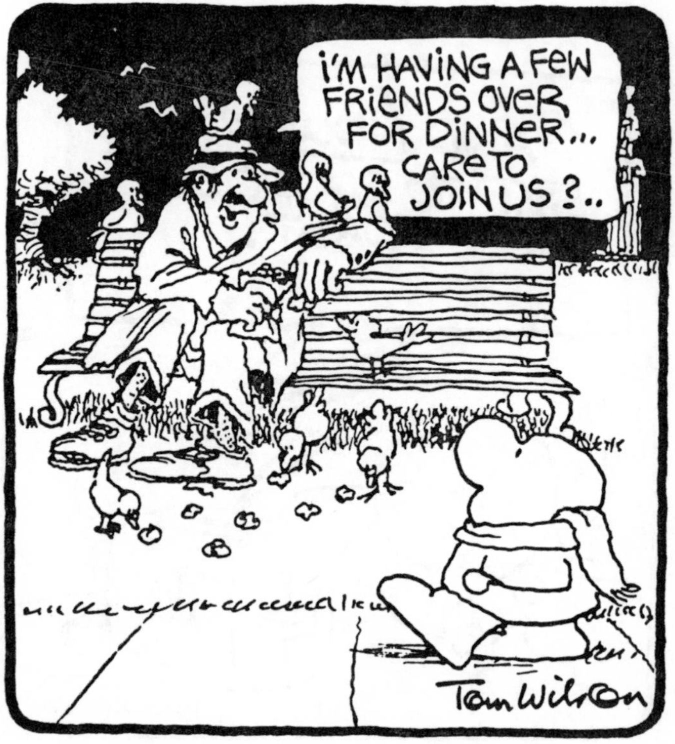
I'M HAVING A FEW FRIENDS OVER FOR DINNER... CARE TO JOIN US?..
Tom Wilson

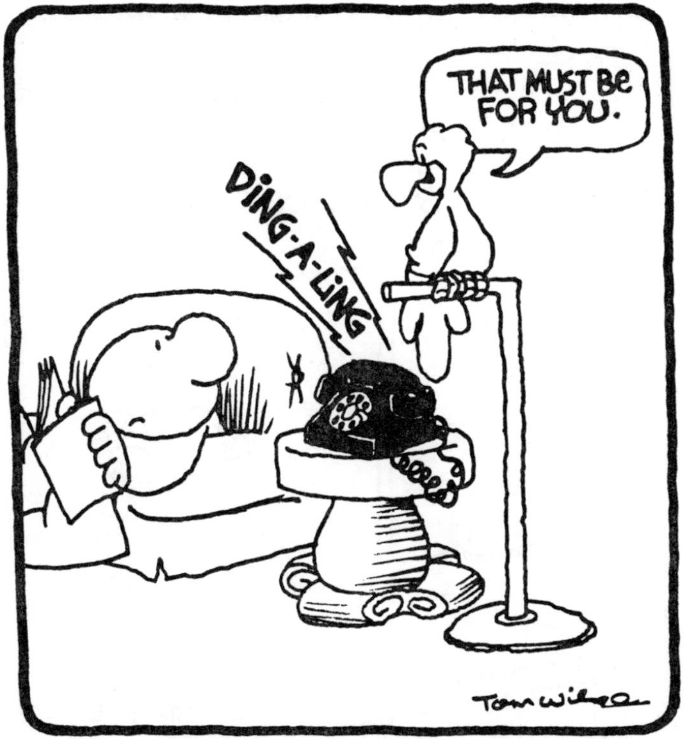
DING-A-LING
THAT MUST BE FOR YOU.
Tom Wilson

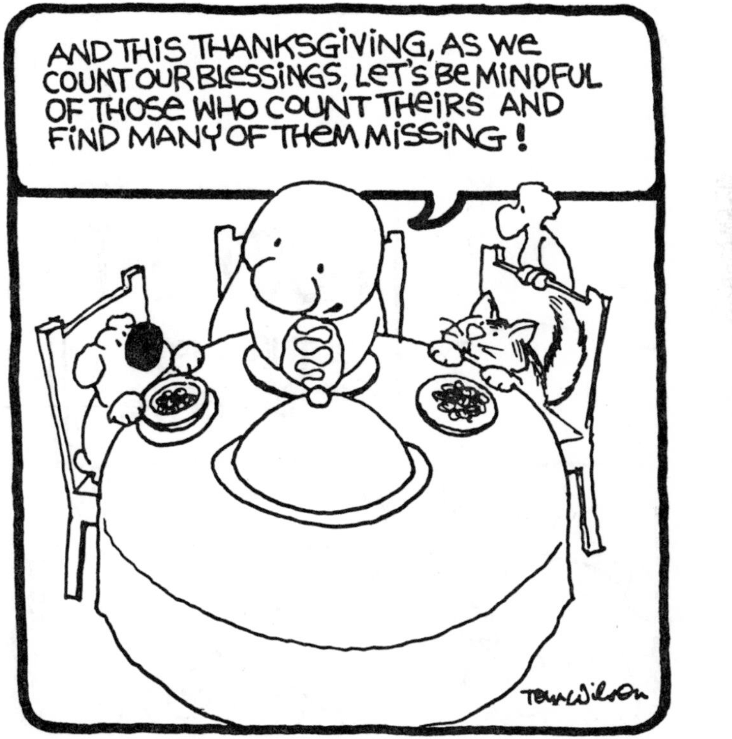
AND THIS THANKSGIVING, AS WE COUNT OUR BLESSINGS, LET'S BE MINDFUL OF THOSE WHO COUNT THEIRS AND FIND MANY OF THEM MISSING!
Tom Wilson

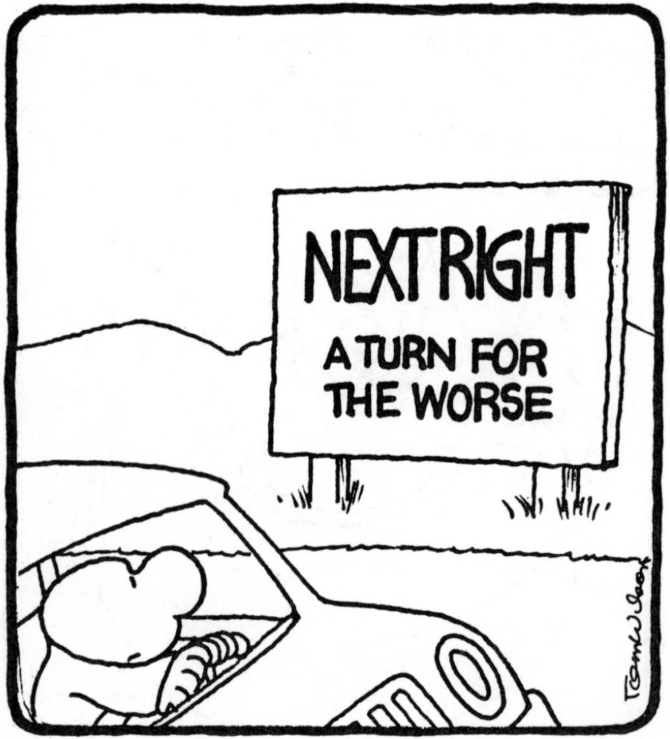
NEXT RIGHT
A TURN FOR THE WORSE
Tom Wilson

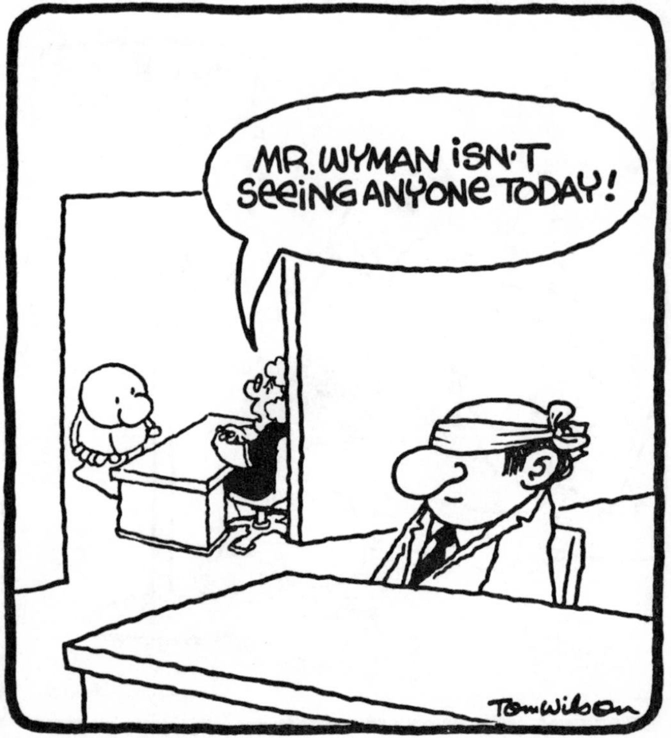
MR. WYMAN ISN'T SEEING ANYONE TODAY!
Tom Wilson

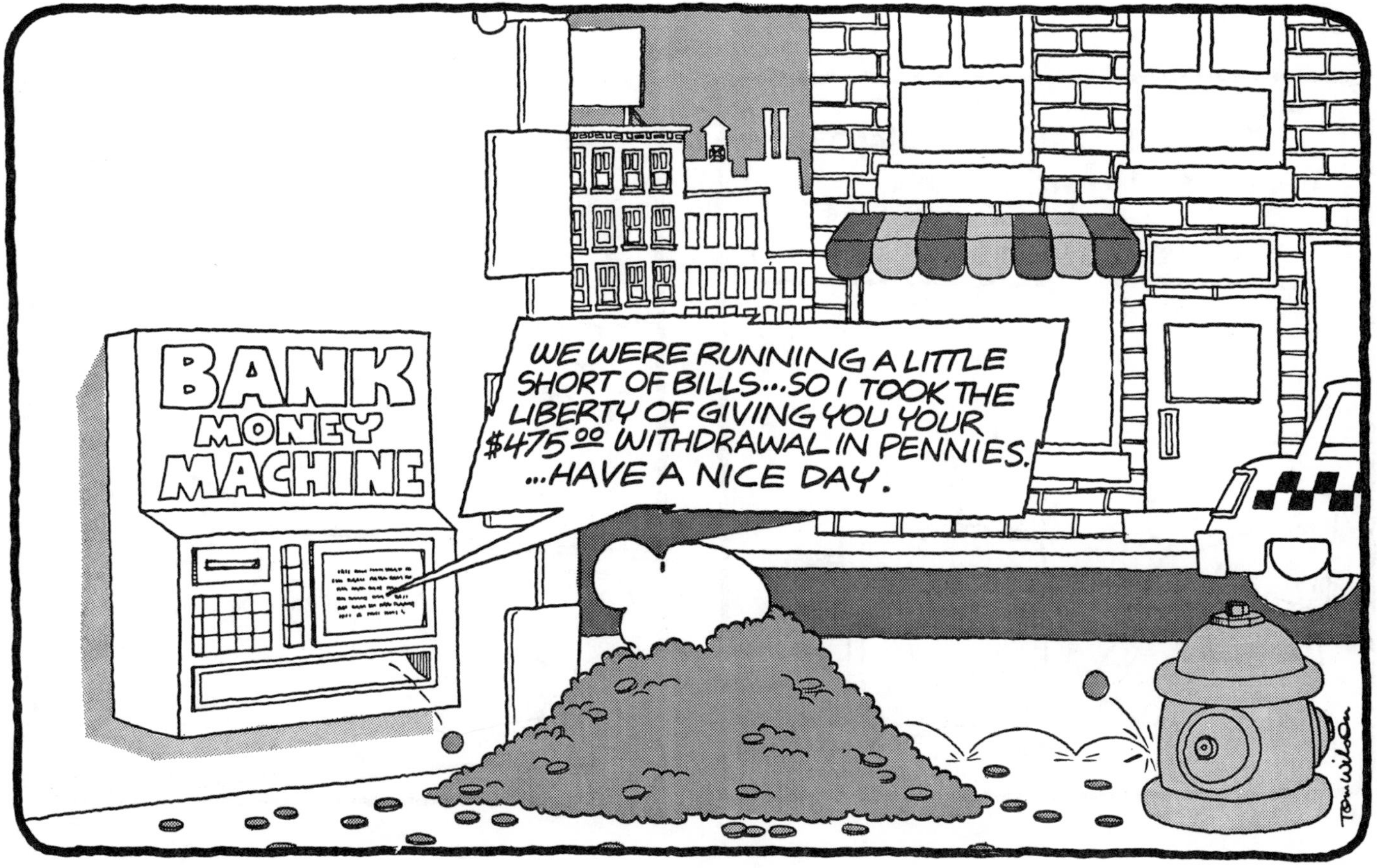
BANK
MONEY
MACHINE
WE WERE RUNNING A LITTLE SHORT OF BILLS...SO I TOOK THE LIBERTY OF GIVING YOU YOUR $475.00 WITHDRAWAL IN PENNIES. ...HAVE A NICE DAY.
Tom Wilson

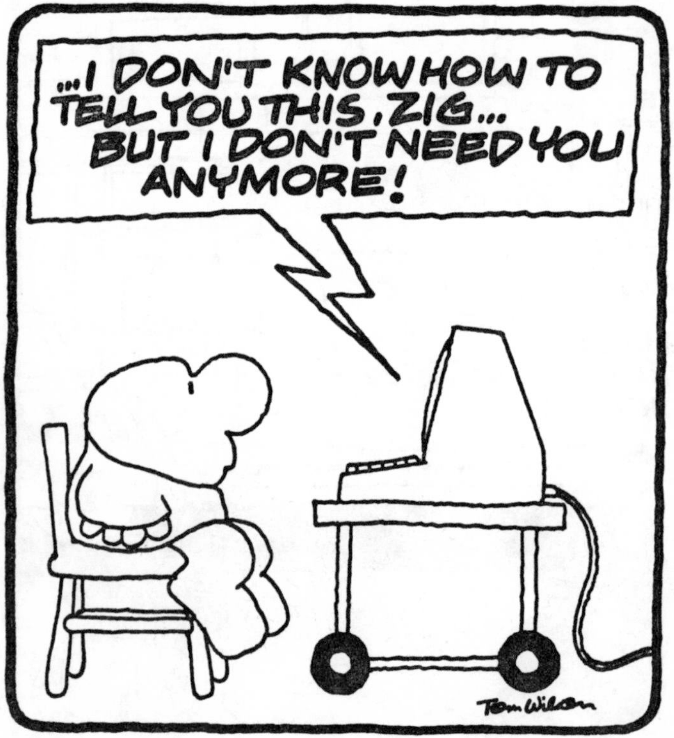
...I DON'T KNOW HOW TO TELL YOU THIS, ZIG... BUT I DON'T NEED YOU ANYMORE!
Tom Wilson

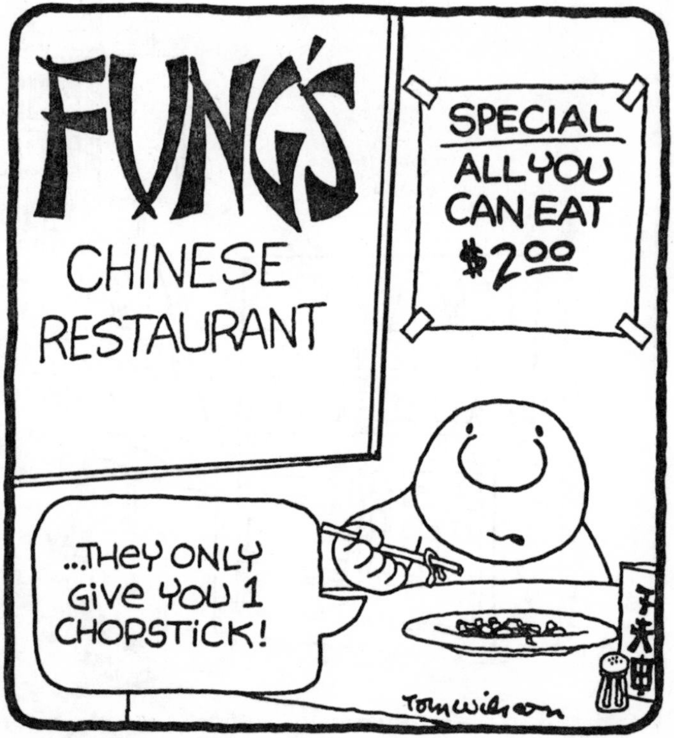
FUNG'S
CHINESE RESTAURANT
SPECIAL
ALL YOU CAN EAT $2.00
...THEY ONLY GIVE YOU 1 CHOPSTICK!
Tom Wilson

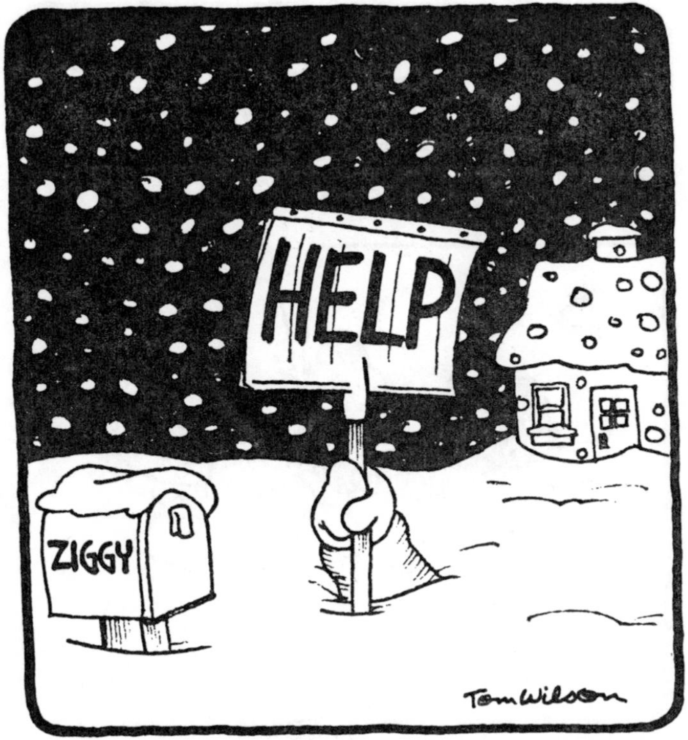
HELP
ZIGGY
Tom Wilson

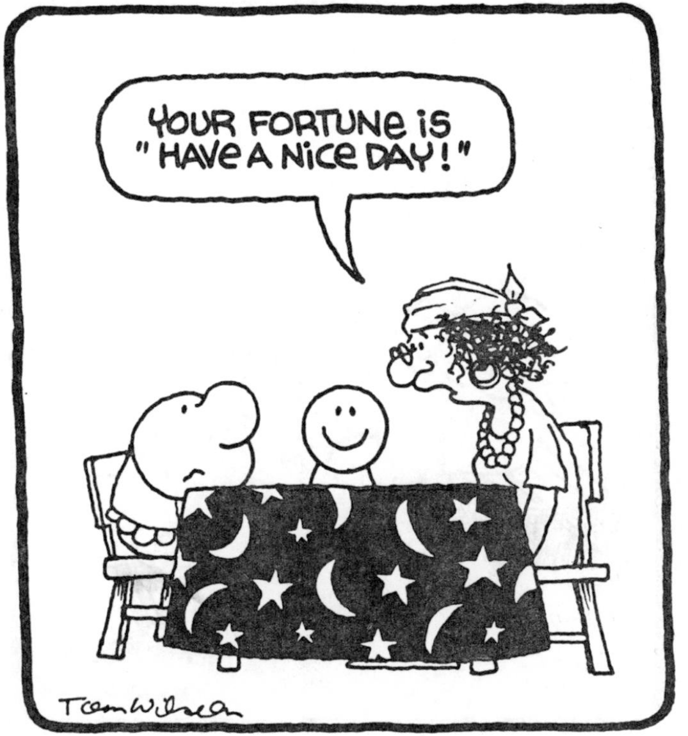
YOUR FORTUNE IS "HAVE A NICE DAY!"
Tom Wilson

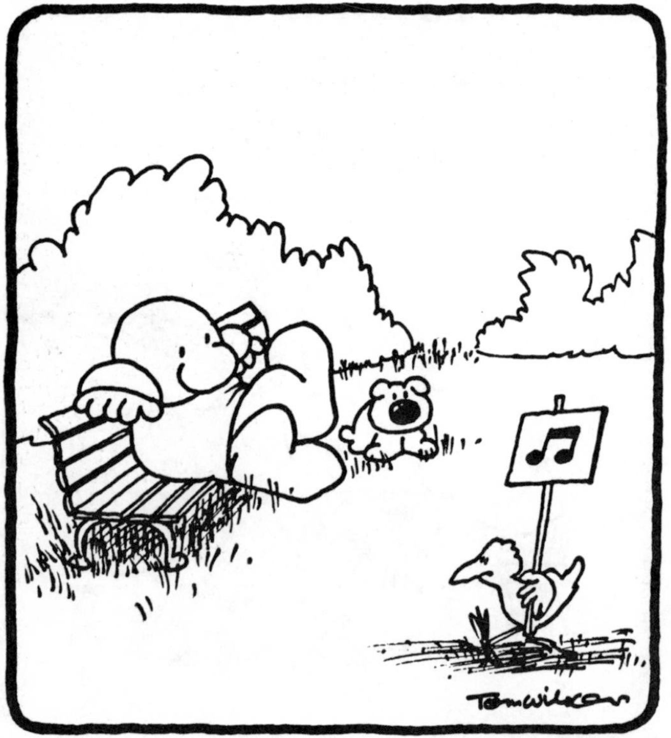

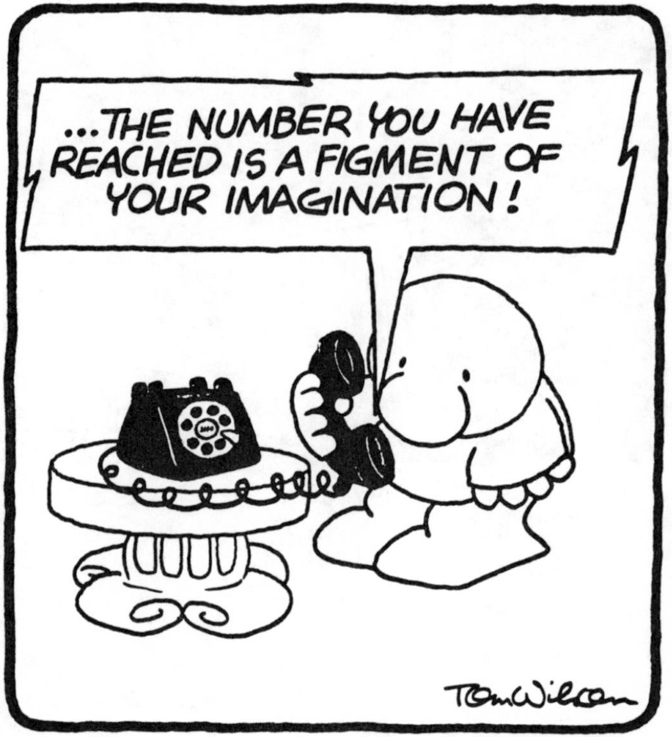
...THE NUMBER YOU HAVE REACHED IS A FIGMENT OF YOUR IMAGINATION!
TOM WILSON

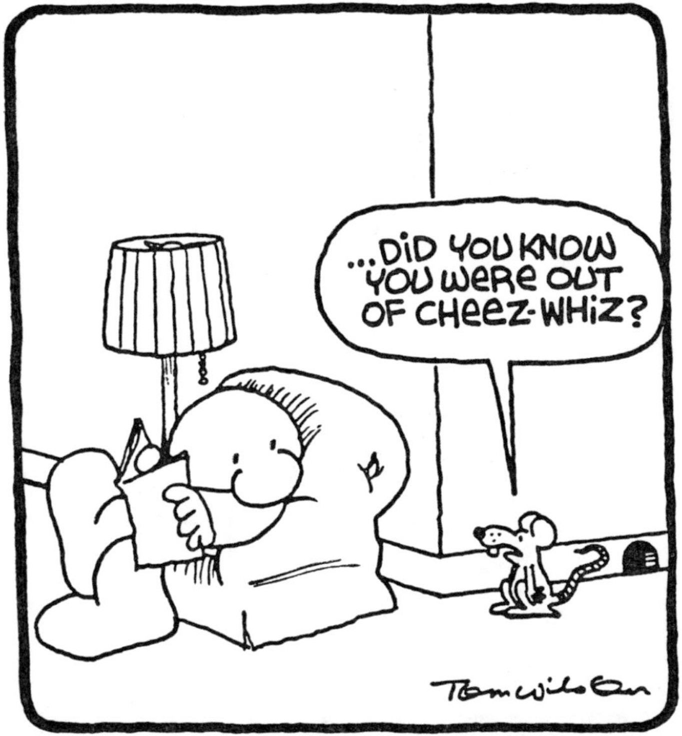
...DID YOU KNOW YOU WERE OUT OF CHEEZ-WHIZ?
Tom Wilson

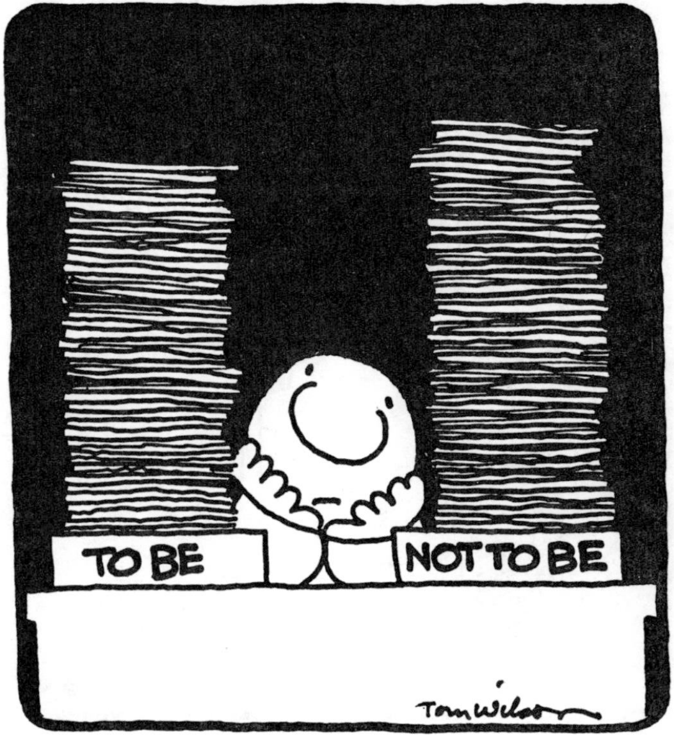
TO BE
NOT TO BE
Tom Wilson

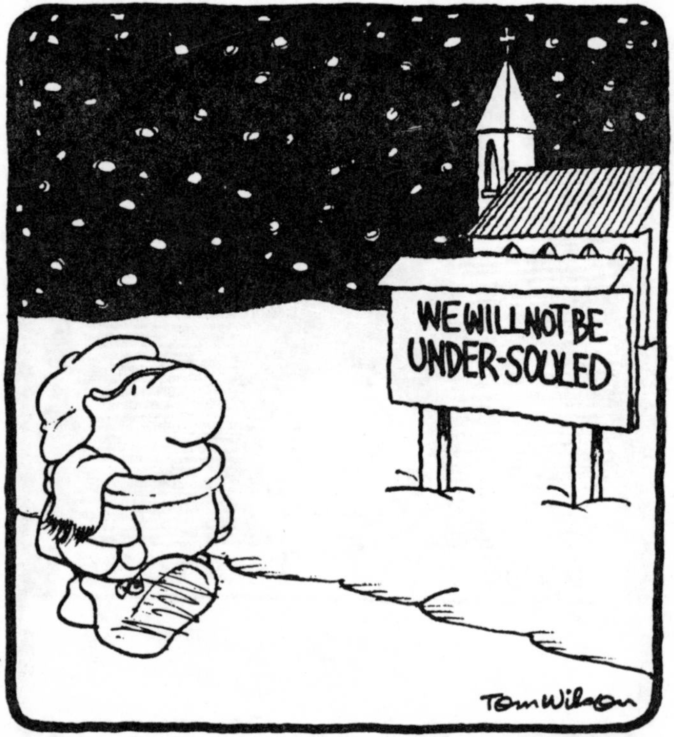
WE WILL NOT BE UNDER-SOULED
Tom Wilson

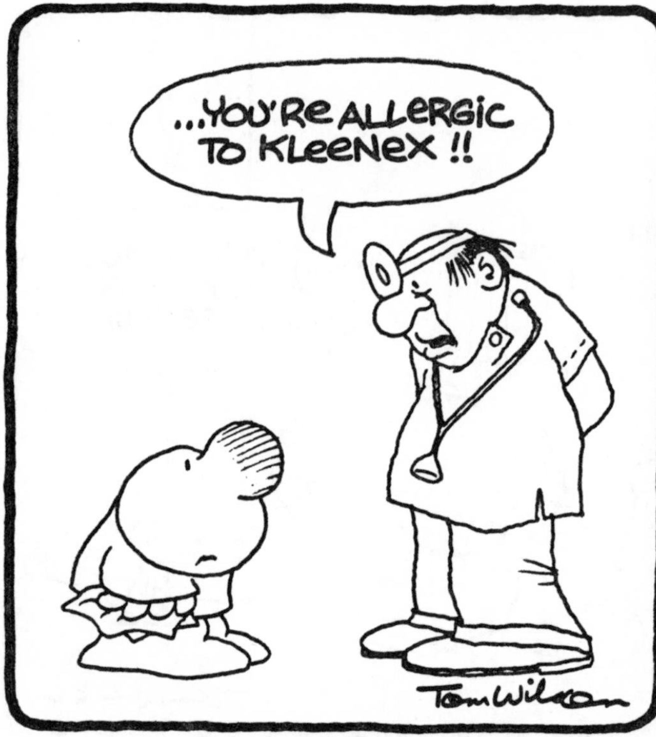
...YOU'RE ALLERGIC TO KLEENEX !!
Tom Wilson

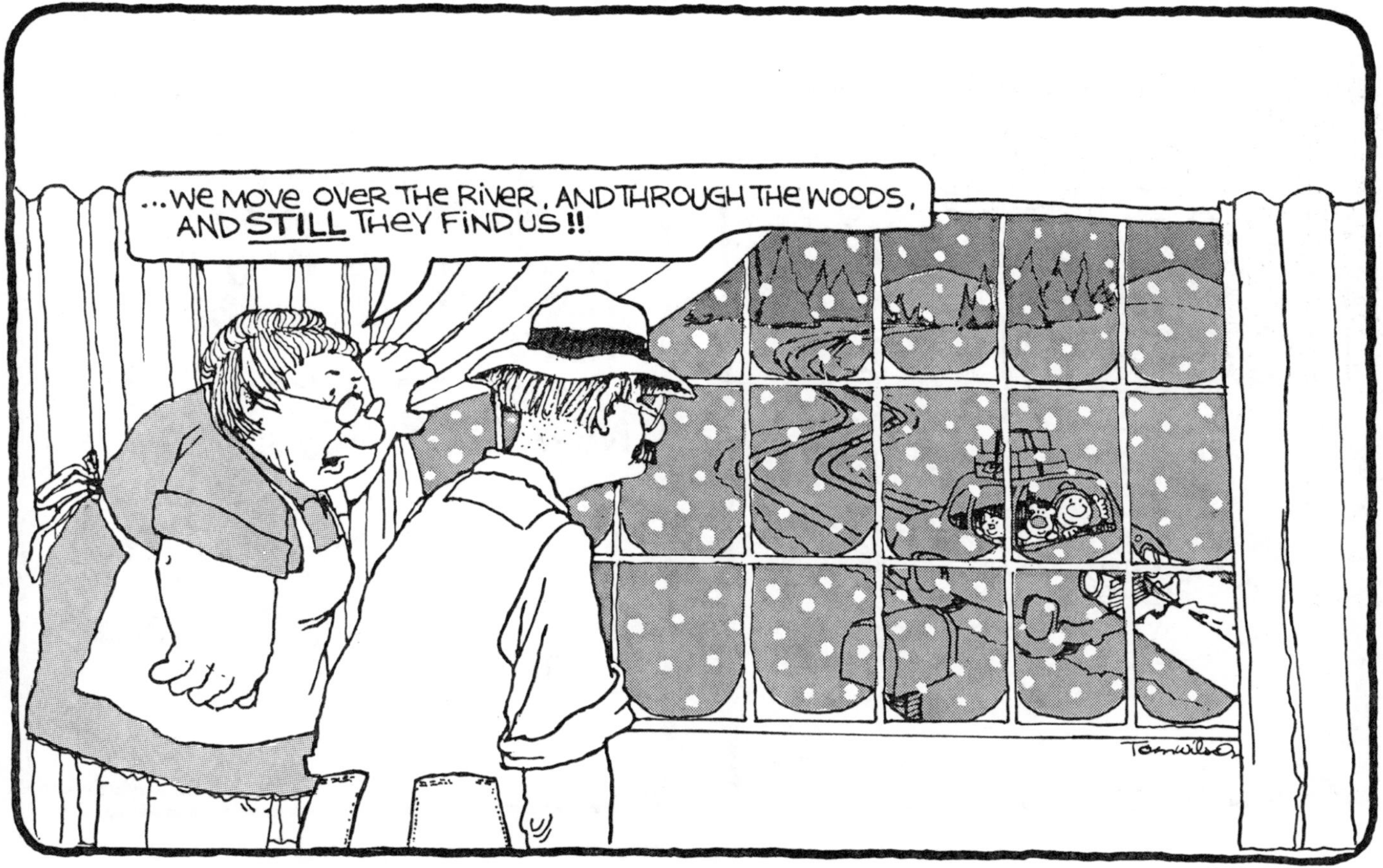
...WE MOVE OVER THE RIVER, AND THROUGH THE WOODS, AND STILL THEY FIND US!!
Tom Wilson

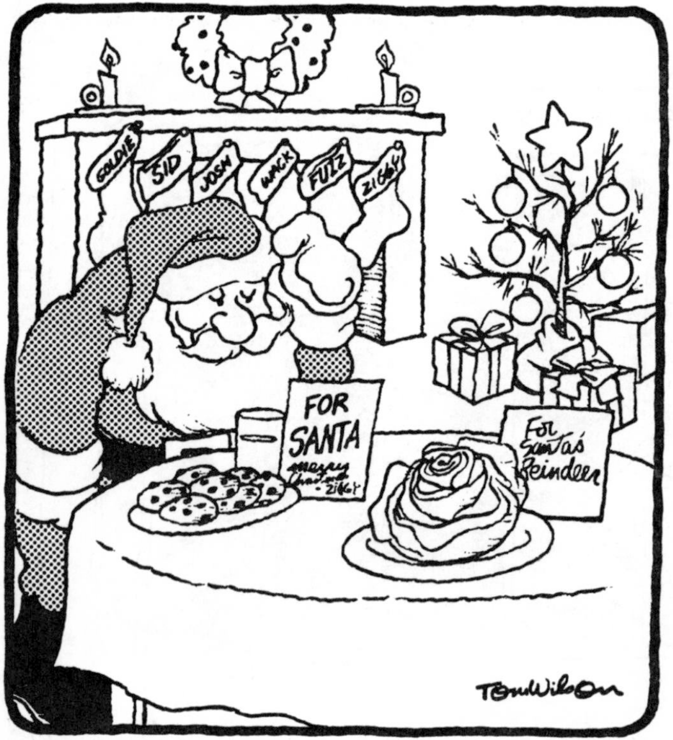
GOLDIE
SID
JOSH
WACK
FUZZ
ZIGGY
FOR SANTA
For Santa's Reindeer
TomWilson

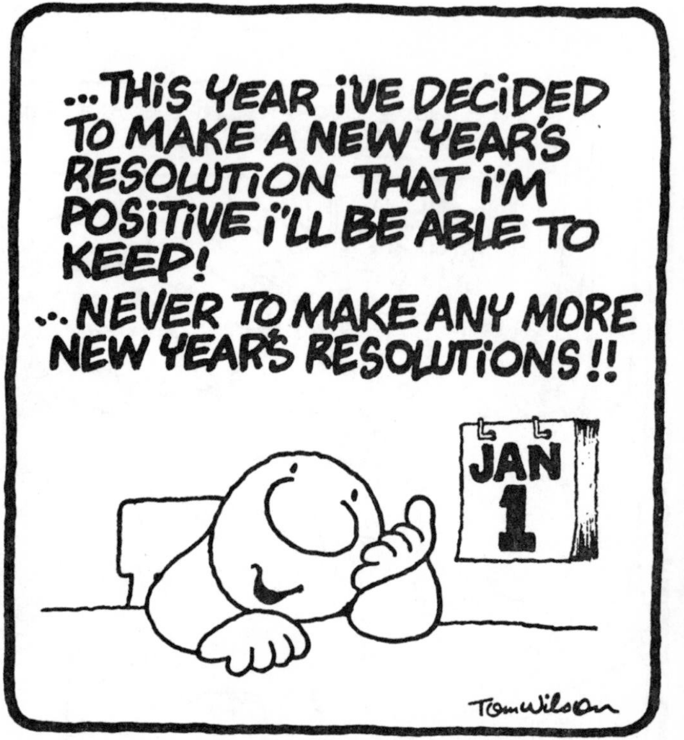
...THIS YEAR I'VE DECIDED TO MAKE A NEW YEAR'S RESOLUTION THAT I'M POSITIVE I'LL BE ABLE TO KEEP!
...NEVER TO MAKE ANY MORE NEW YEAR'S RESOLUTIONS!!
JAN
1
TomWilson

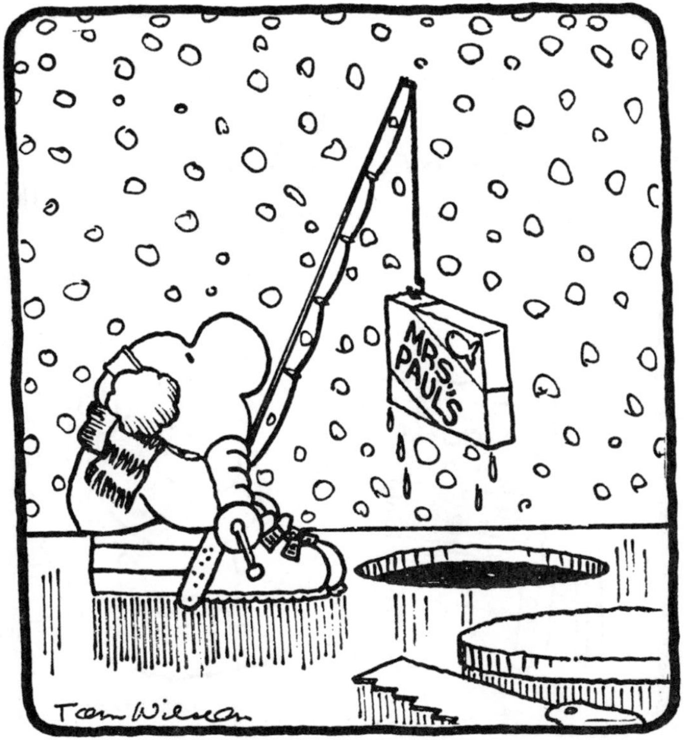
MRS. PAUL'S
Tom Wilson

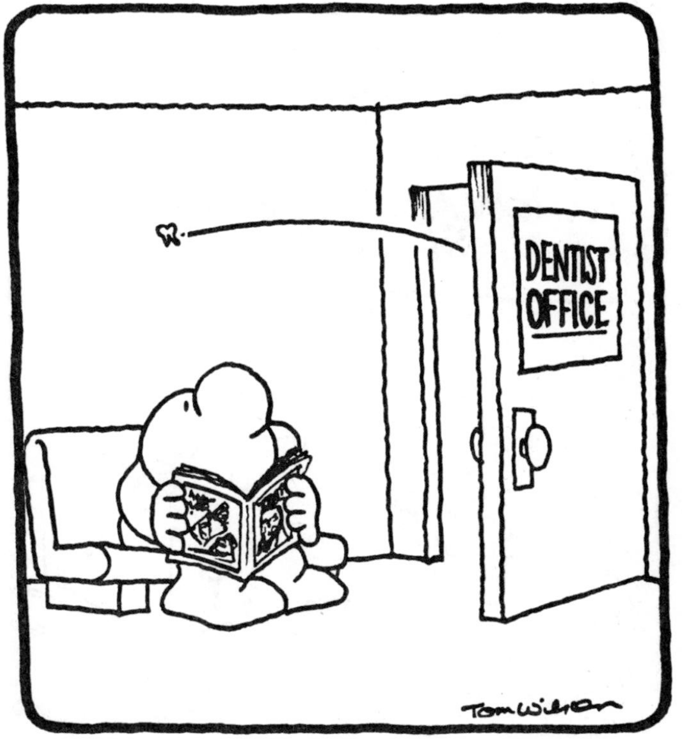
DENTIST OFFICE
Tom Wilson

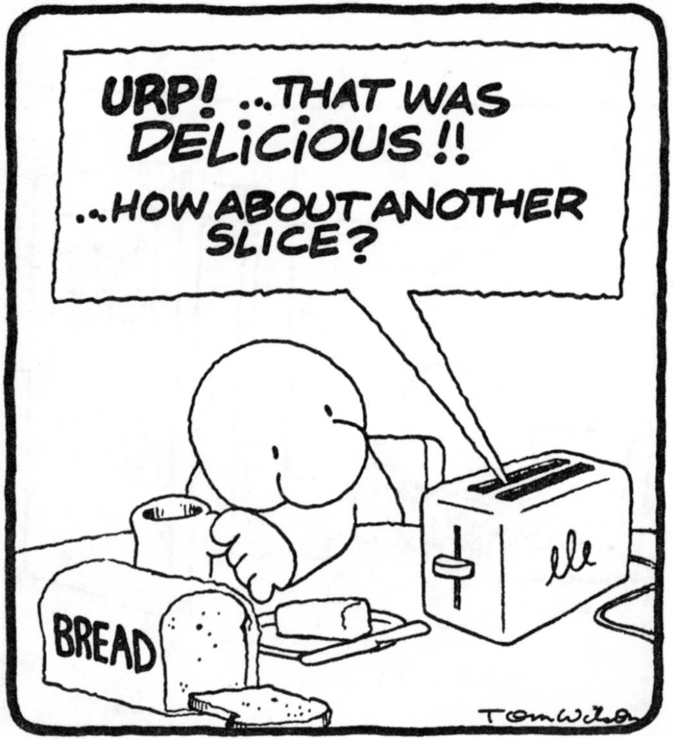
URP! ...THAT WAS DELICIOUS !!
...HOW ABOUT ANOTHER SLICE?
BREAD

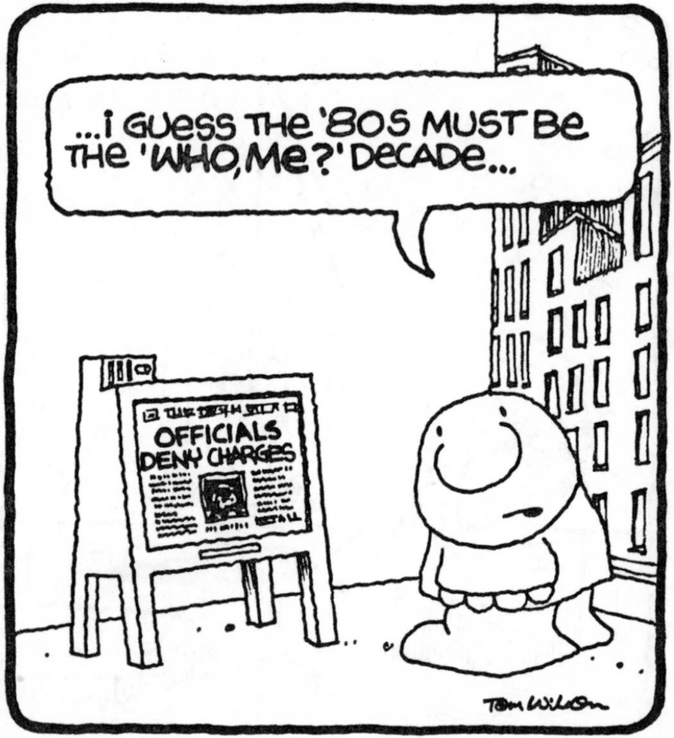
...I GUESS THE '80S MUST BE THE 'WHO, ME?' DECADE...
OFFICIALS DENY CHARGES

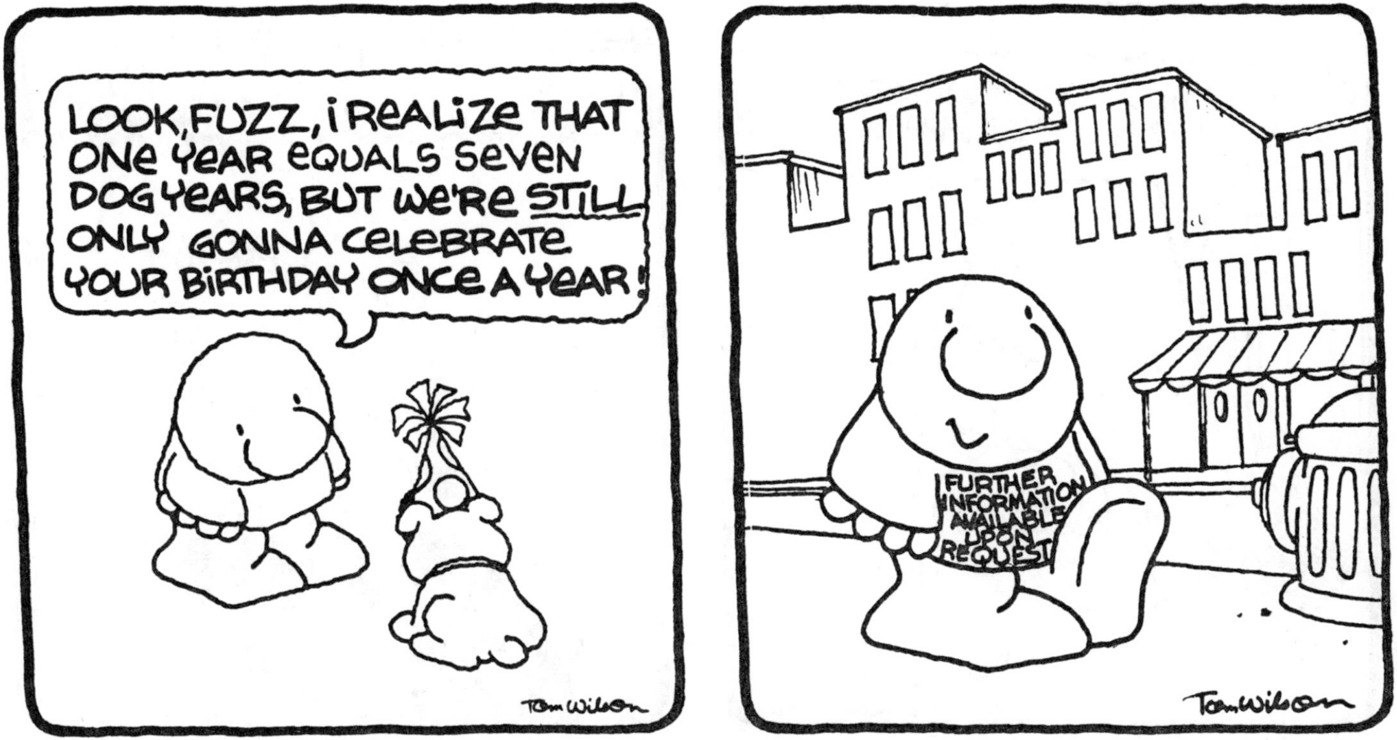
LOOK, FUZZ, I REALIZE THAT ONE YEAR EQUALS SEVEN DOG YEARS, BUT WE'RE STILL ONLY GONNA CELEBRATE YOUR BIRTHDAY ONCE A YEAR!
Tom Wilson
FURTHER INFORMATION AVAILABLE UPON REQUEST
Tom Wilson

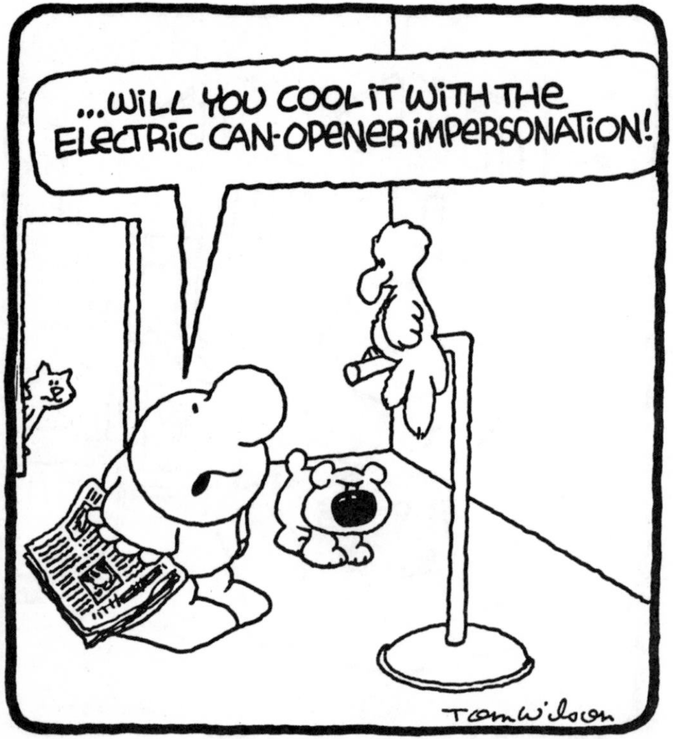
...WILL YOU COOL IT WITH THE ELECTRIC CAN-OPENER IMPERSONATION!
Tom Wilson

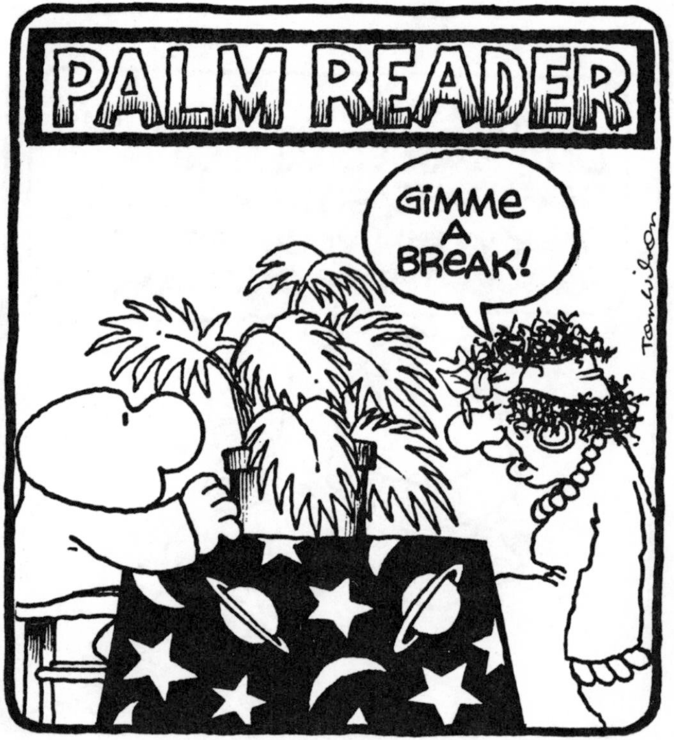
PALM READER
GIMME A BREAK!
Tom Wilson

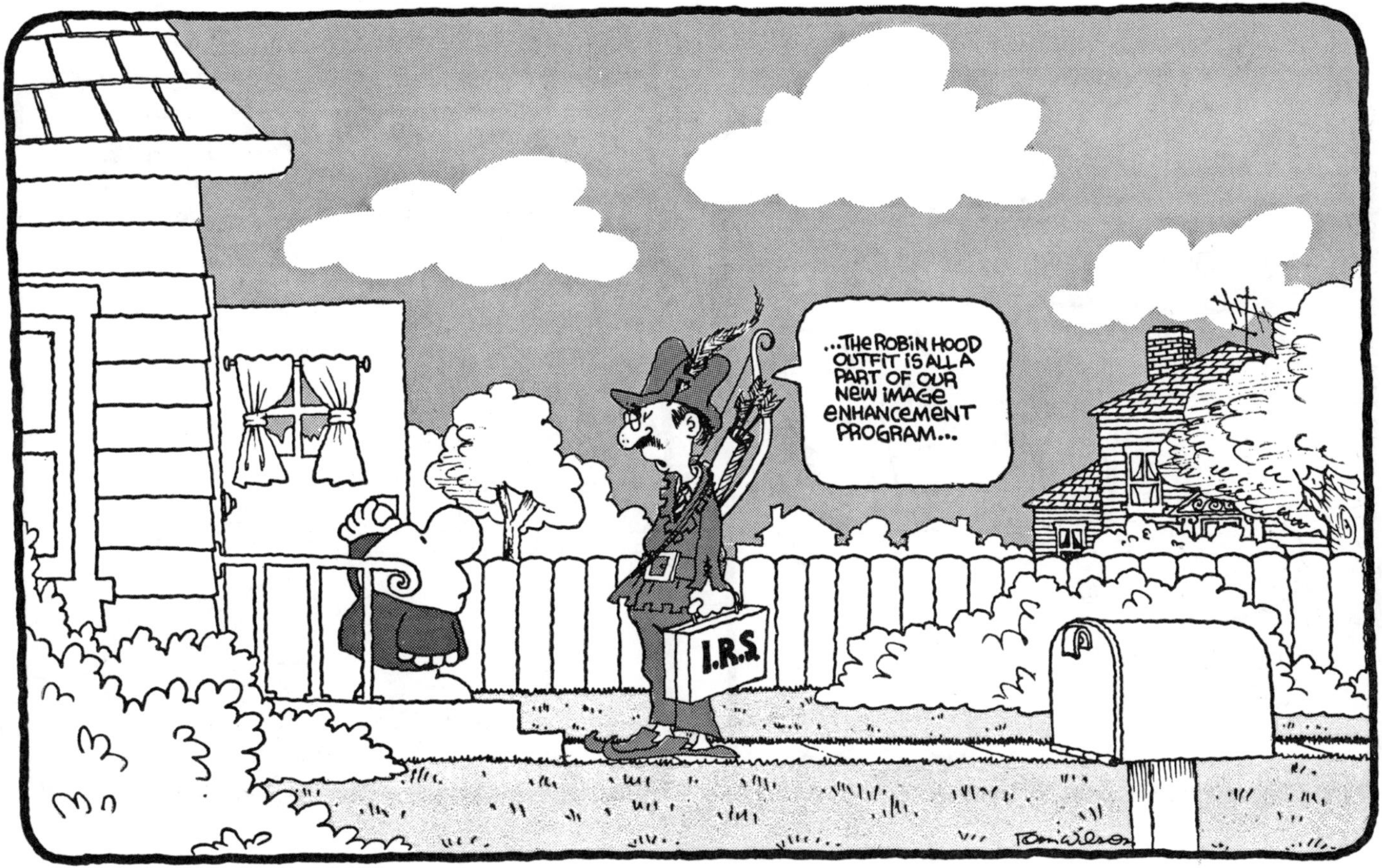
...THE ROBIN HOOD OUTFIT IS ALL A PART OF OUR NEW IMAGE ENHANCEMENT PROGRAM...
I.R.S.
Tom Wilson

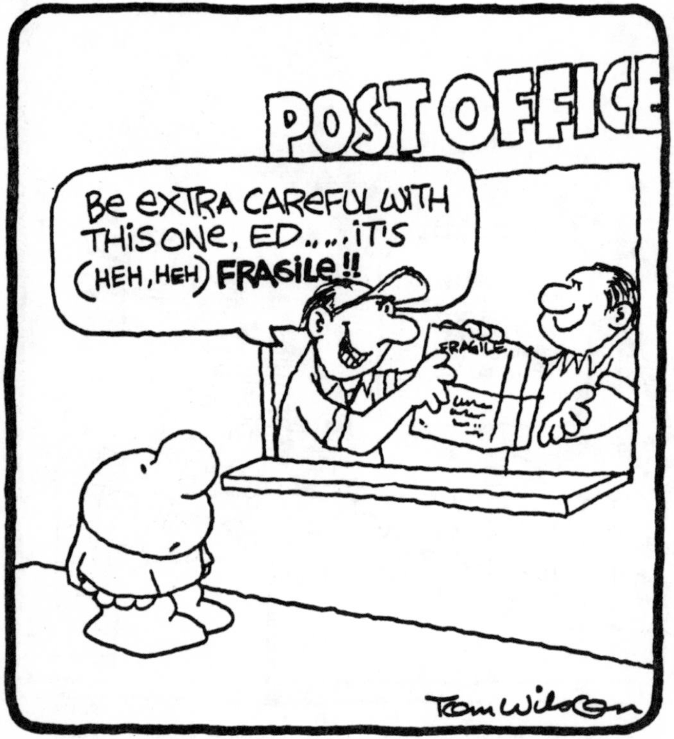
POST OFFICE
Be EXTRA CAREFUL WITH THIS ONE, ED......IT'S (HEH, HEH) FRAGILE!!
FRAGILE
Tom Wilson

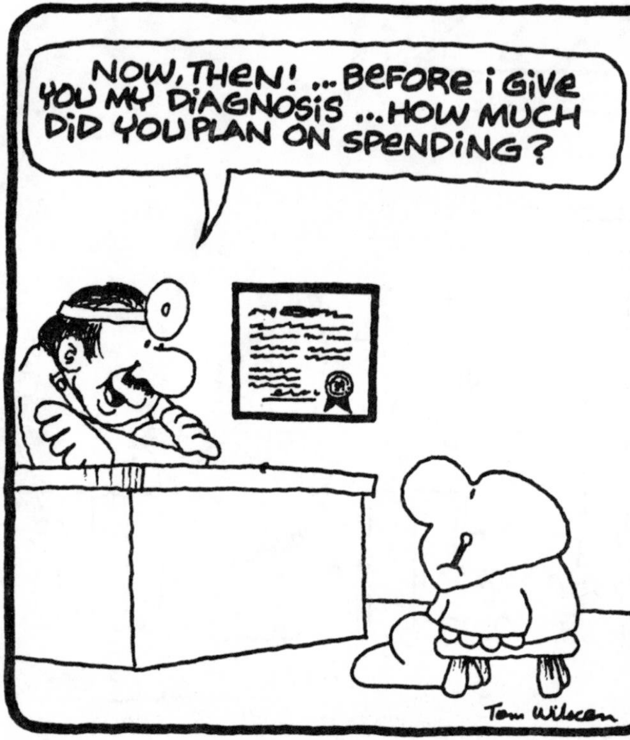
NOW, THEN! ...BEFORE I GIVE YOU MY DIAGNOSIS ...HOW MUCH DID YOU PLAN ON SPENDING?
Tom Wilson

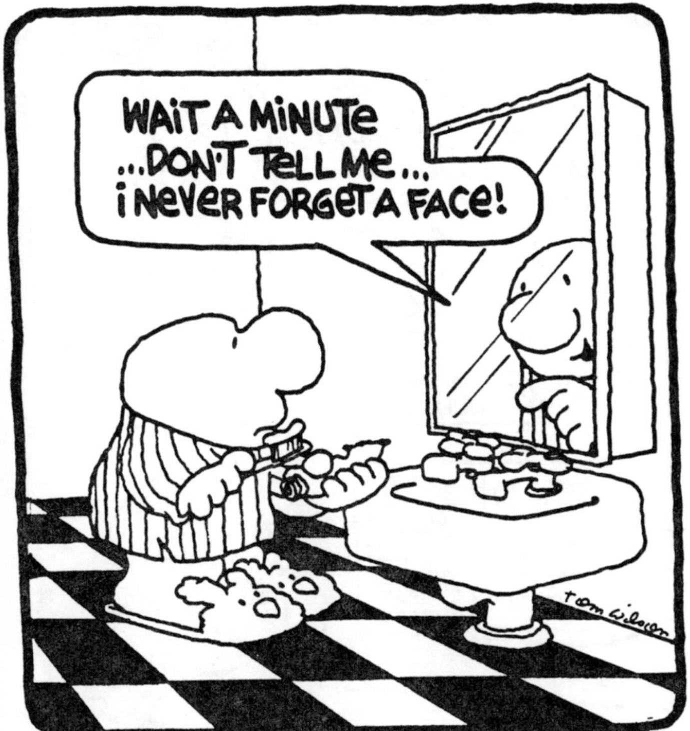
WAIT A MINUTE ...DON'T TELL ME... I NEVER FORGET A FACE!
Tom Wilson

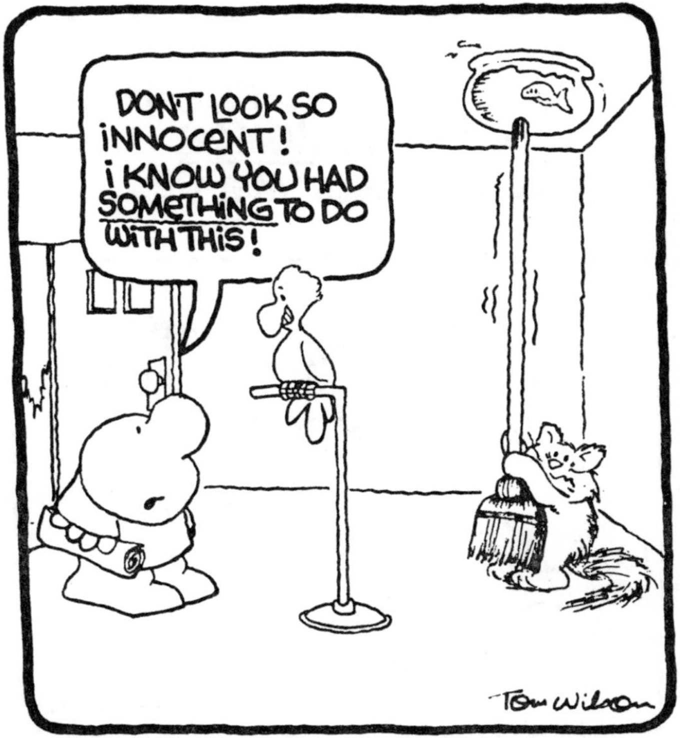
DON'T LOOK SO INNOCENT! I KNOW YOU HAD SOMETHING TO DO WITH THIS!
Tom Wilson

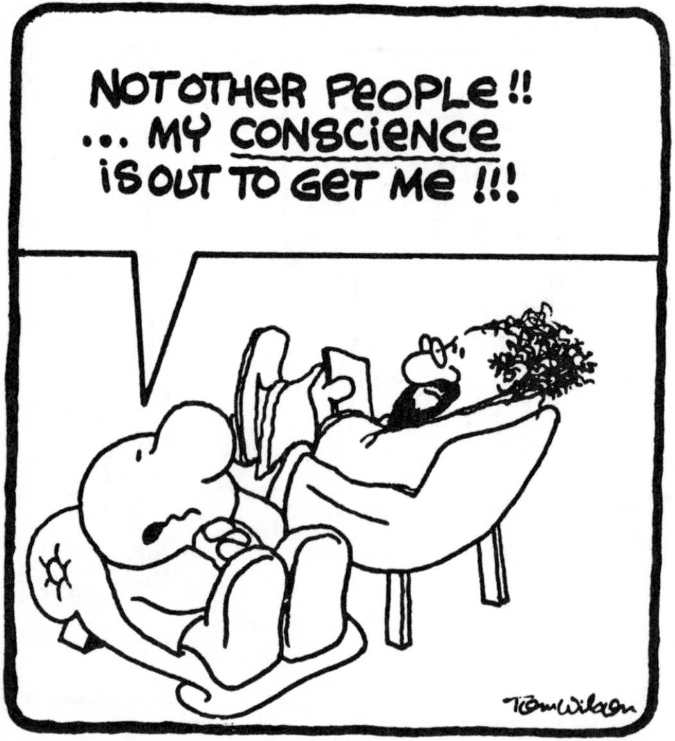
NOT OTHER PEOPLE!! ... MY CONSCIENCE IS OUT TO GET ME!!!
Tom Wilson

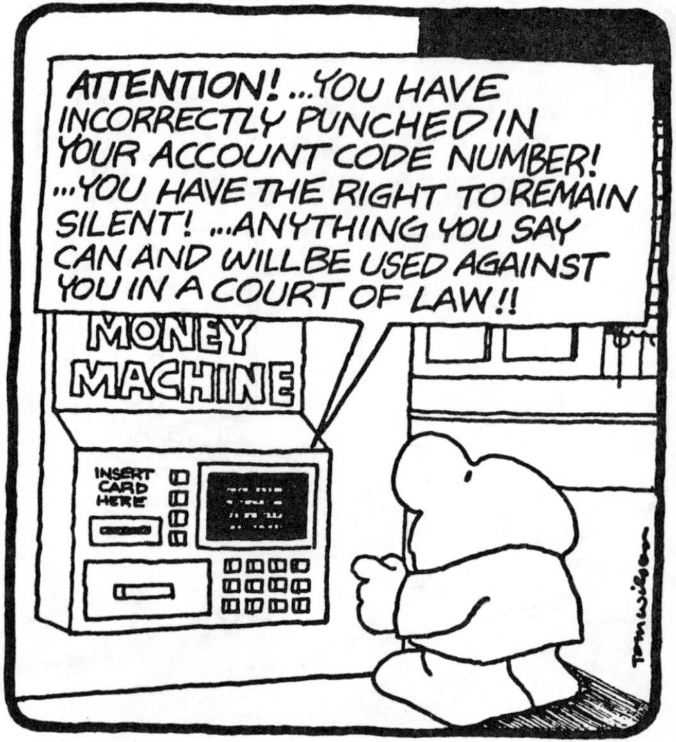
ATTENTION! ...YOU HAVE INCORRECTLY PUNCHED IN YOUR ACCOUNT CODE NUMBER! ...YOU HAVE THE RIGHT TO REMAIN SILENT! ...ANYTHING YOU SAY CAN AND WILL BE USED AGAINST YOU IN A COURT OF LAW!!
MONEY MACHINE
INSERT CARD HERE
Tom Wilson

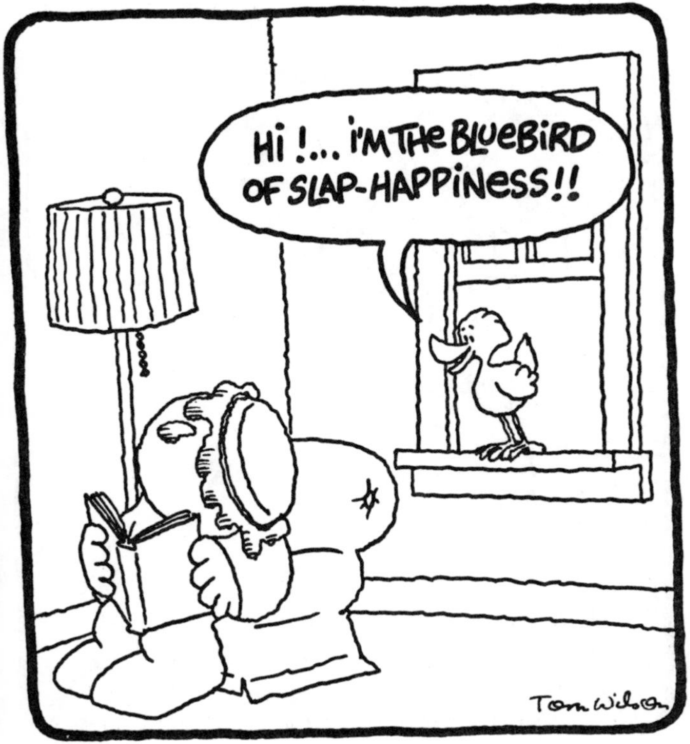
HI !... I'M THE BLUEBIRD OF SLAP-HAPPINESS !!
Tom Wilson

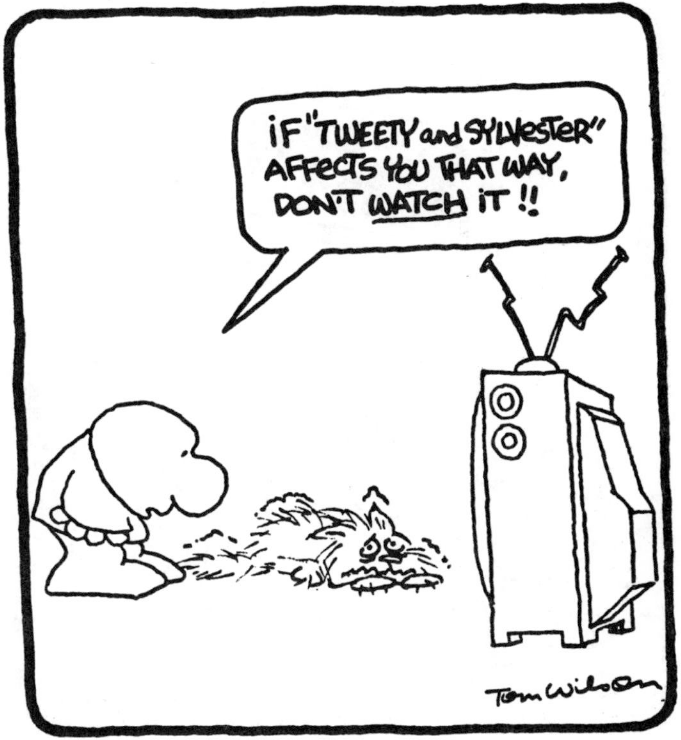
IF "TWEETY and SYLVESTER" AFFECTS YOU THAT WAY, DON'T WATCH IT !!
Tom Wilson

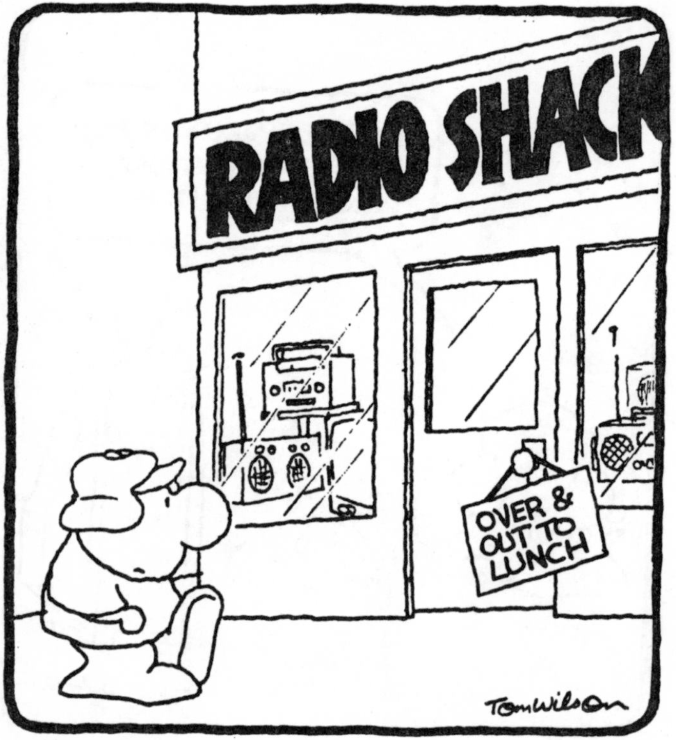
RADIO SHACK
OVER & OUT TO LUNCH
Tom Wilson

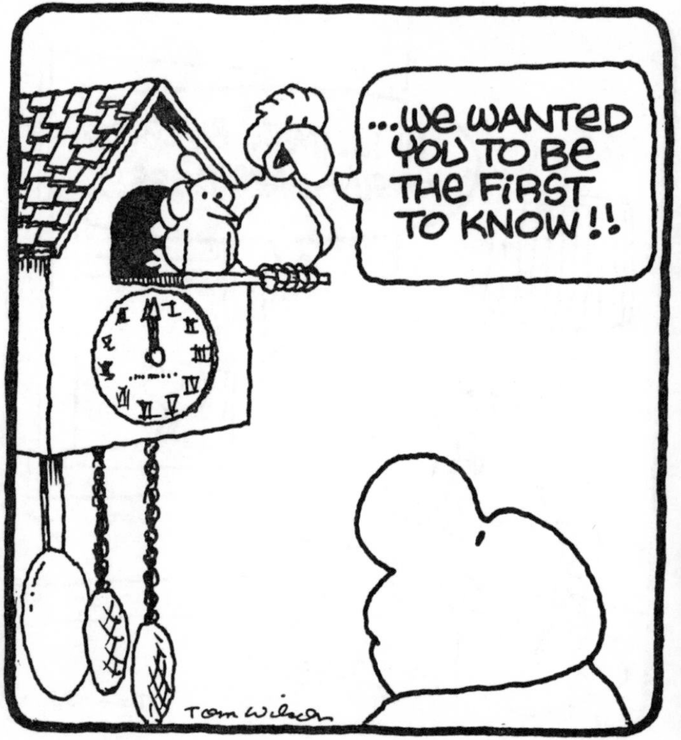
...WE WANTED YOU TO BE THE FIRST TO KNOW!!
Tom Wilson

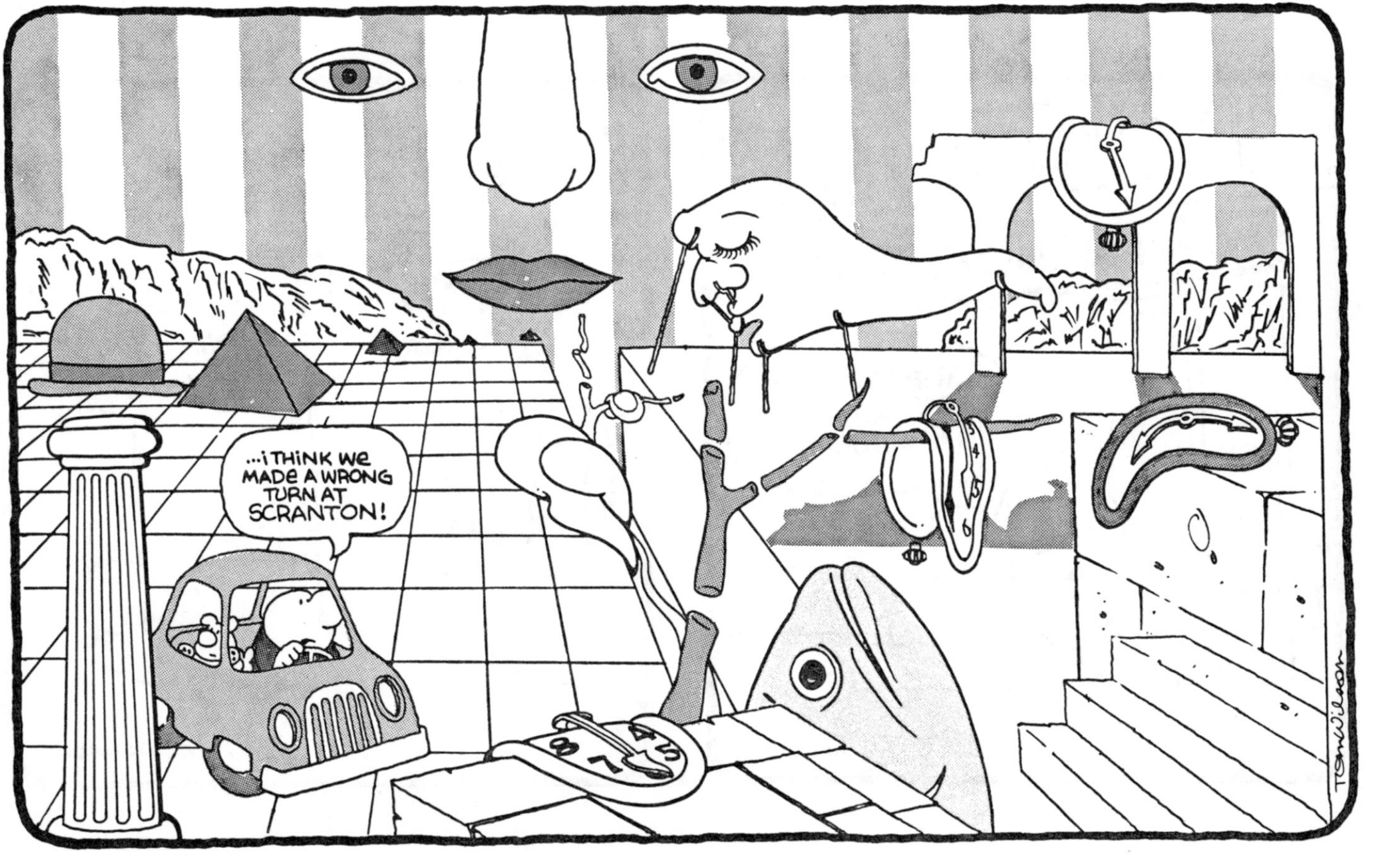
...i THINK WE MADE A WRONG TURN AT SCRANTON!
Tom Wilson

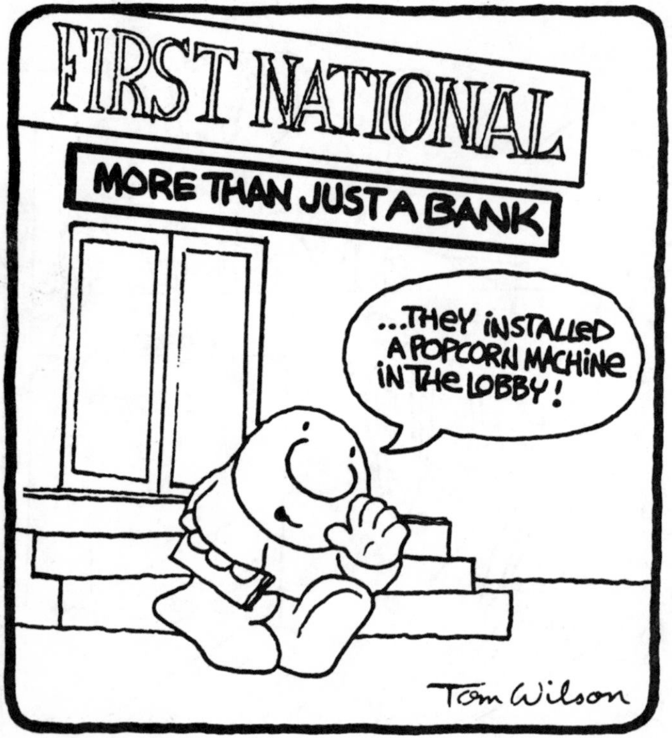
FIRST NATIONAL
MORE THAN JUST A BANK
...THEY INSTALLED A POPCORN MACHINE IN THE LOBBY!
Tom Wilson

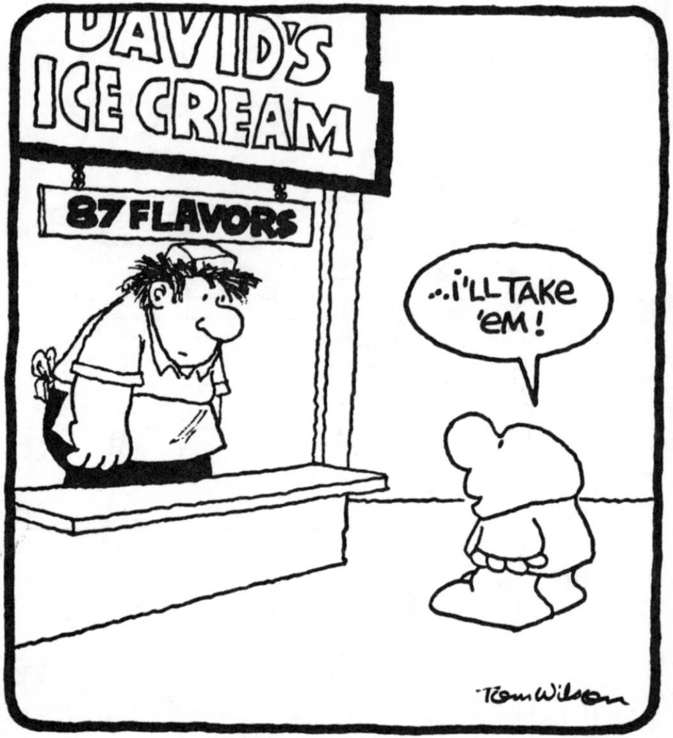
DAVID'S ICE CREAM
87 FLAVORS
..I'LL TAKE 'EM!
Tom Wilson

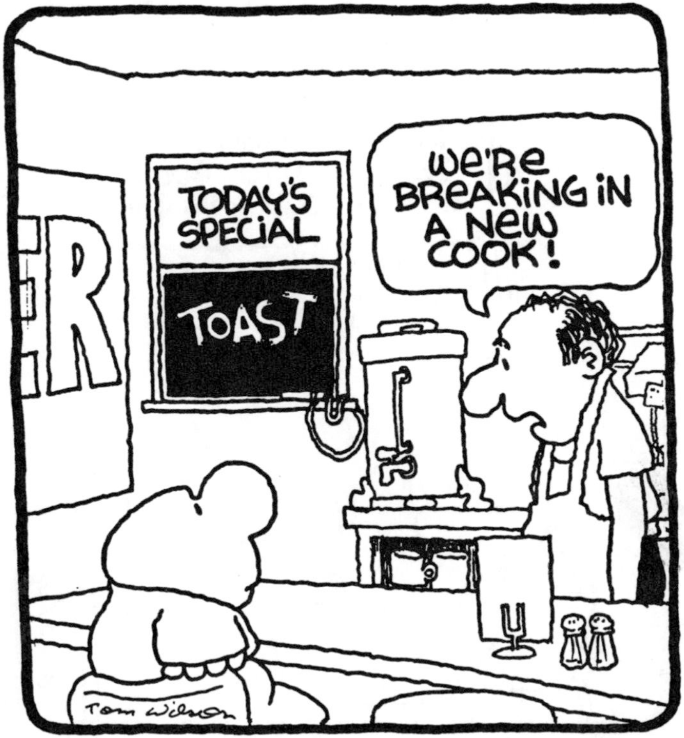
TODAY'S SPECIAL
TOAST
WE'RE BREAKING IN A NEW COOK!
Tom Wilson

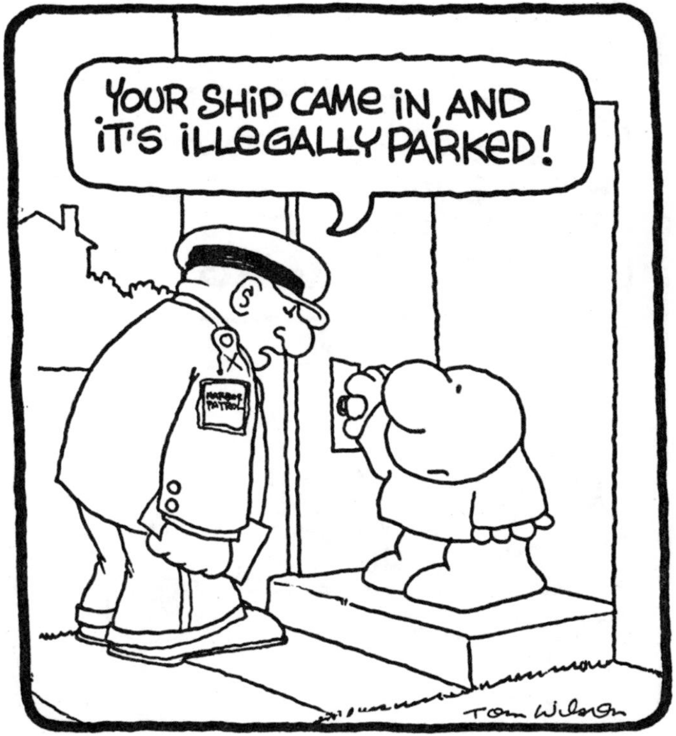
YOUR SHIP CAME IN, AND IT'S ILLEGALLY PARKED!
Tom Wilson

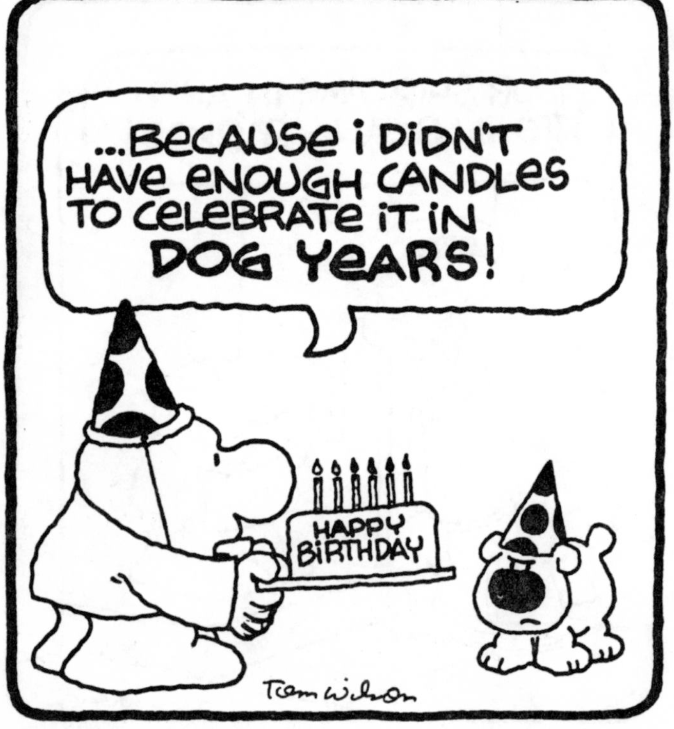
...BECAUSE I DIDN'T HAVE ENOUGH CANDLES TO CELEBRATE IT IN DOG YEARS!
HAPPY BIRTHDAY
Tom Wilson

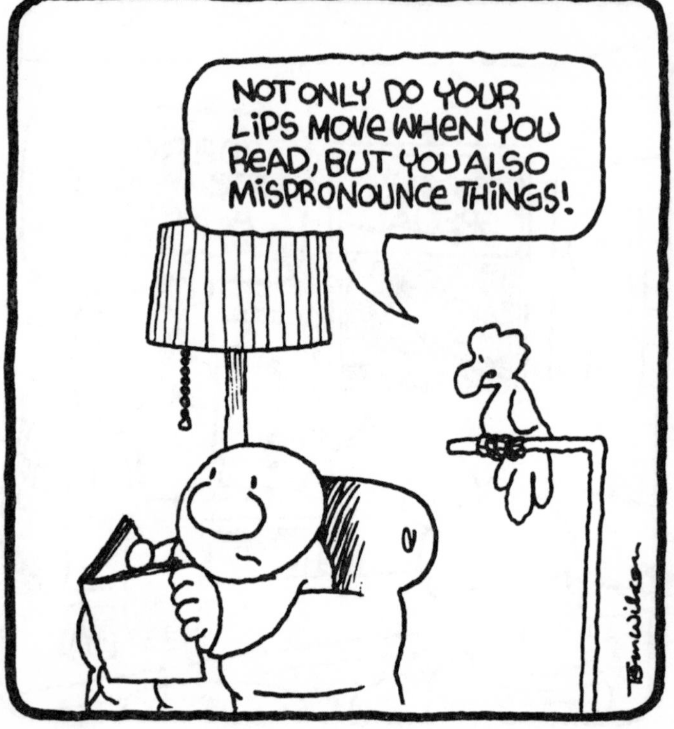
NOT ONLY DO YOUR LIPS MOVE WHEN YOU READ, BUT YOU ALSO MISPRONOUNCE THINGS!
Tom Wilson

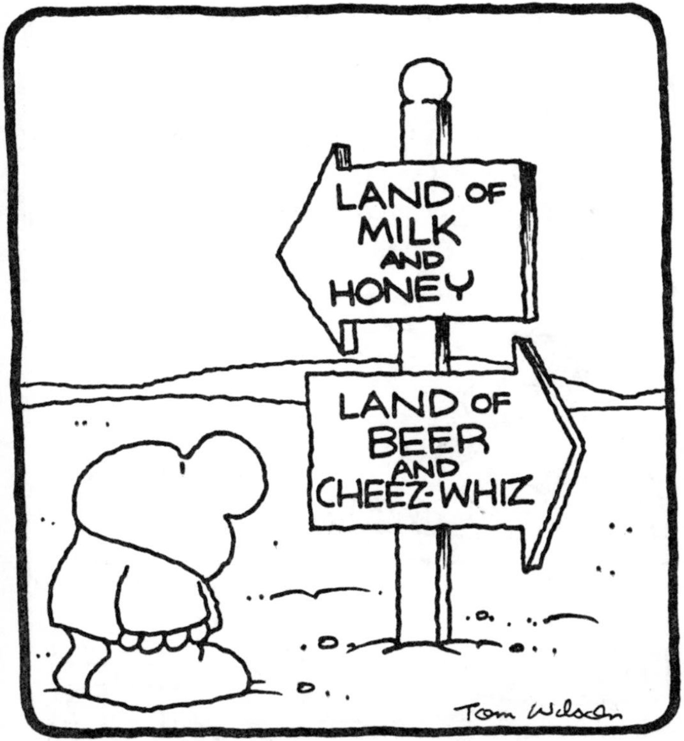
LAND OF MILK AND HONEY
LAND OF BEER AND CHEEZ-WHIZ
Tom Wilson

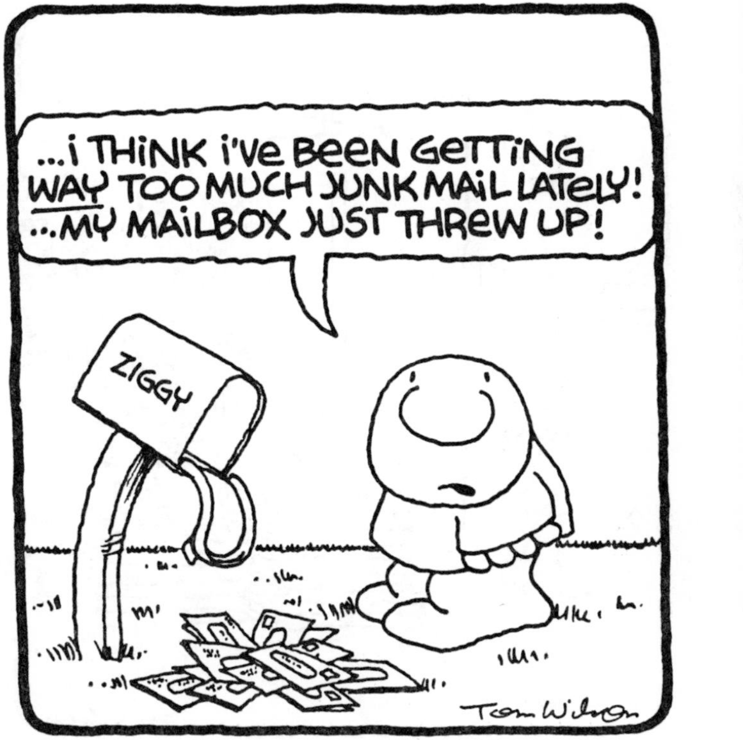
...i THINK i've BEEN GETTING WAY TOO MUCH JUNK MAIL LATELY! ...MY MAILBOX JUST THREW UP!
ZIGGY
Tom Wilson

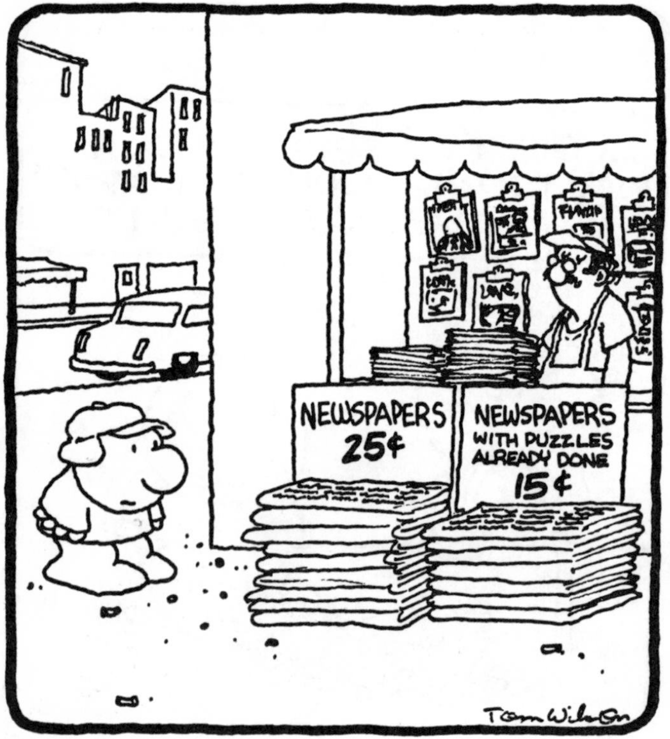
NEWSPAPERS
25¢
NEWSPAPERS
WITH PUZZLES ALREADY DONE
15¢

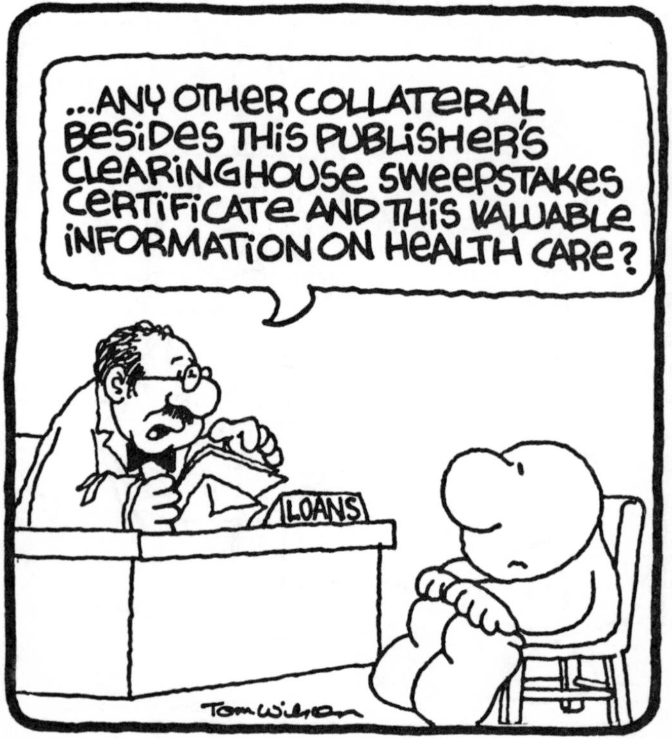
...ANY OTHER COLLATERAL BESIDES THIS PUBLISHER'S CLEARINGHOUSE SWEEPSTAKES CERTIFICATE AND THIS VALUABLE INFORMATION ON HEALTH CARE?
LOANS

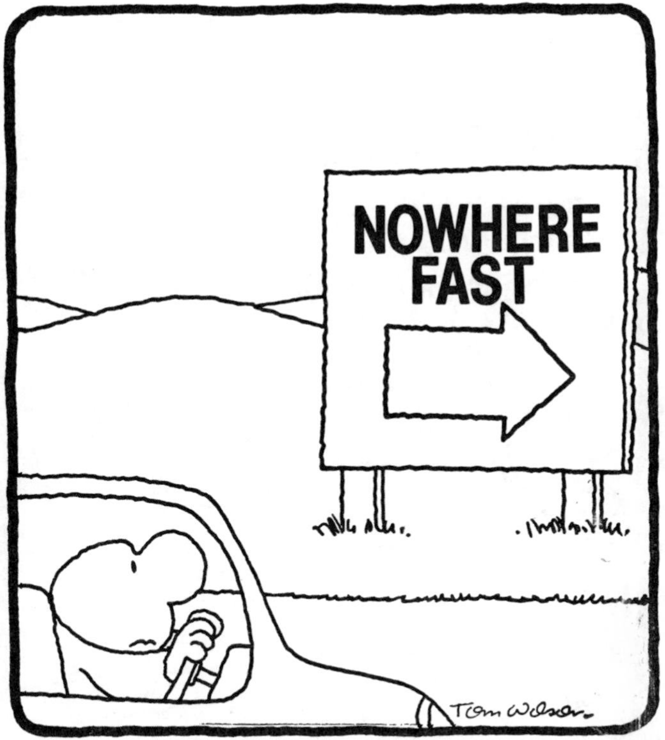
NOWHERE FAST
Tom Wilson

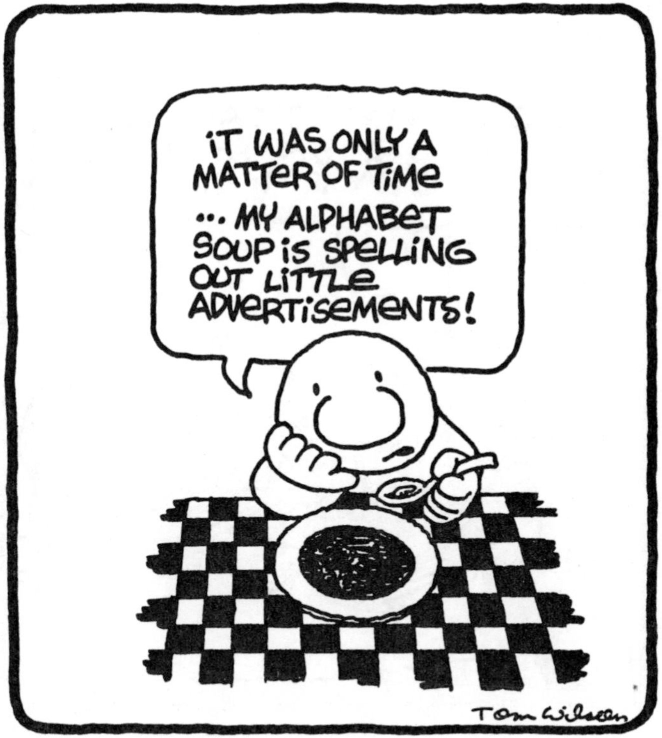
IT WAS ONLY A MATTER OF TIME ... MY ALPHABET SOUP IS SPELLING OUT LITTLE ADVERTISEMENTS!
Tom Wilson

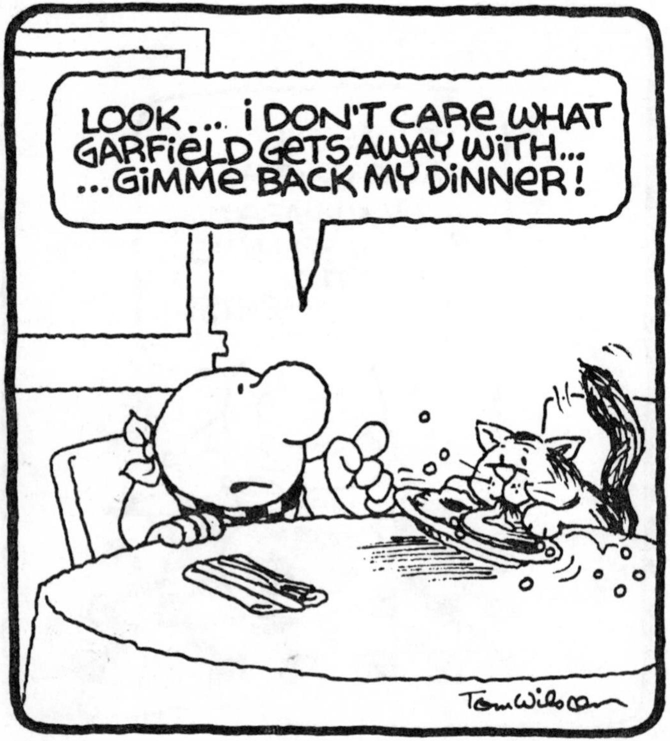
LOOK.... I DON'T CARE WHAT GARFIELD GETS AWAY WITH... ...GIMME BACK MY DINNER!
Tom Wilson

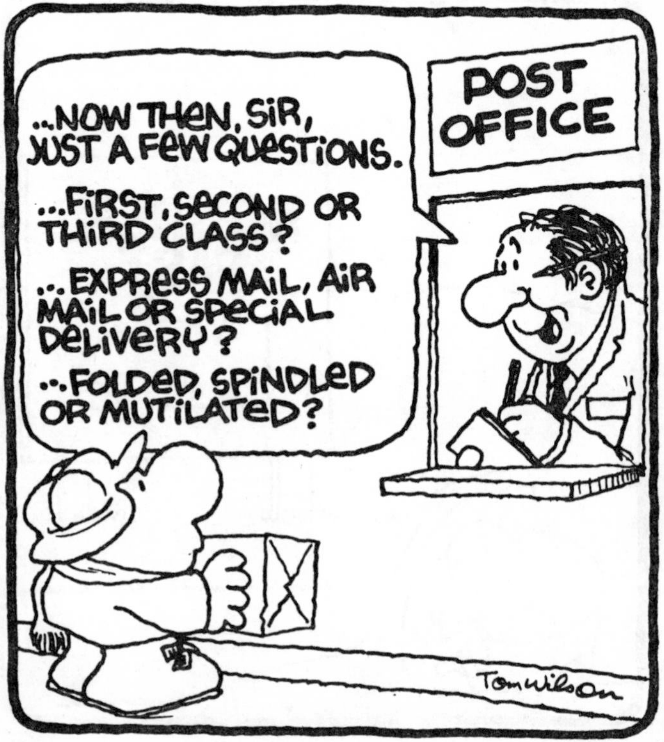
POST OFFICE
...NOW THEN, SIR, JUST A FEW QUESTIONS.
...FIRST, SECOND OR THIRD CLASS?
...EXPRESS MAIL, AIR MAIL OR SPECIAL DELIVERY?
...FOLDED, SPINDLED OR MUTILATED?
Tom Wilson

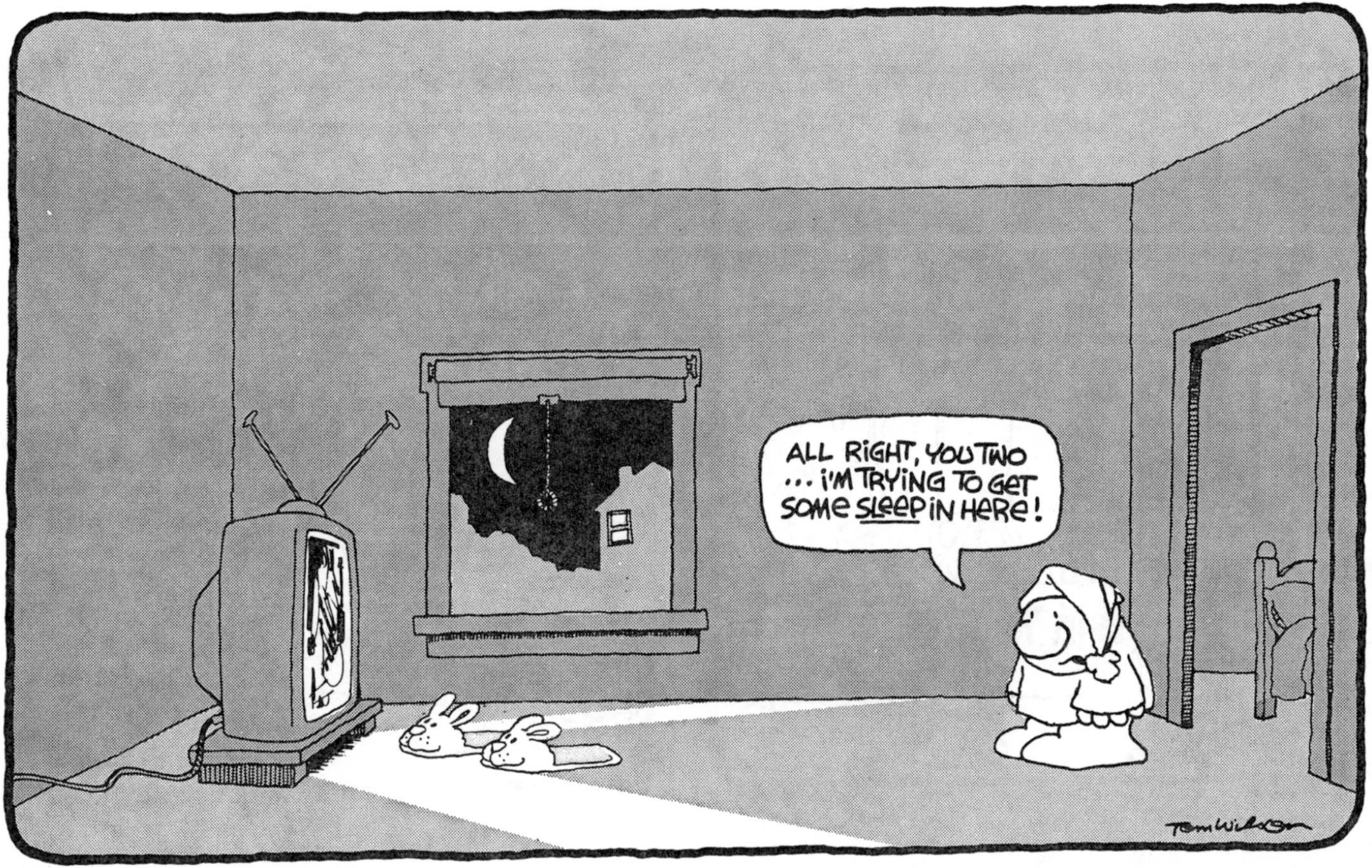
ALL RIGHT, YOU TWO ... I'M TRYING TO GET SOME SLEEP IN HERE!
Tom Wilson

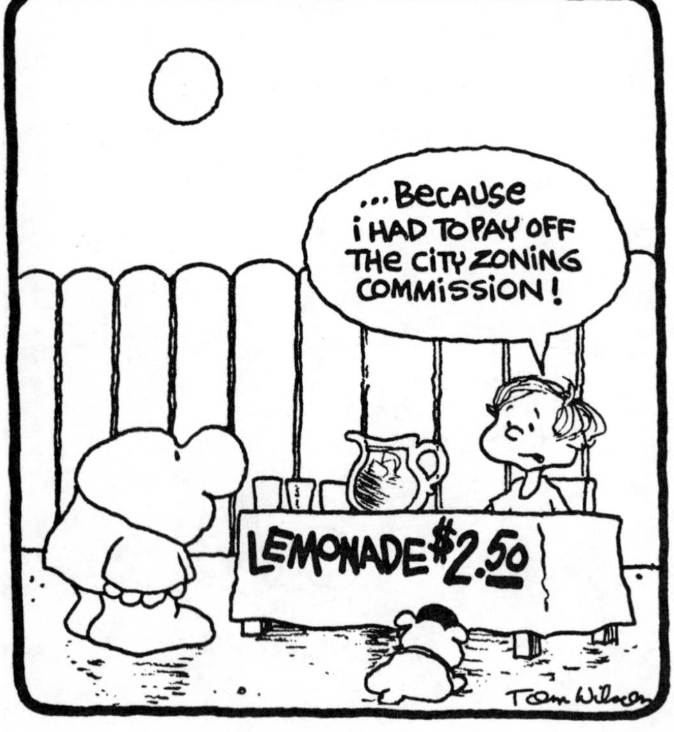
...BECAUSE I HAD TO PAY OFF THE CITY ZONING COMMISSION!
LEMONADE $2.50
Tom Wilson

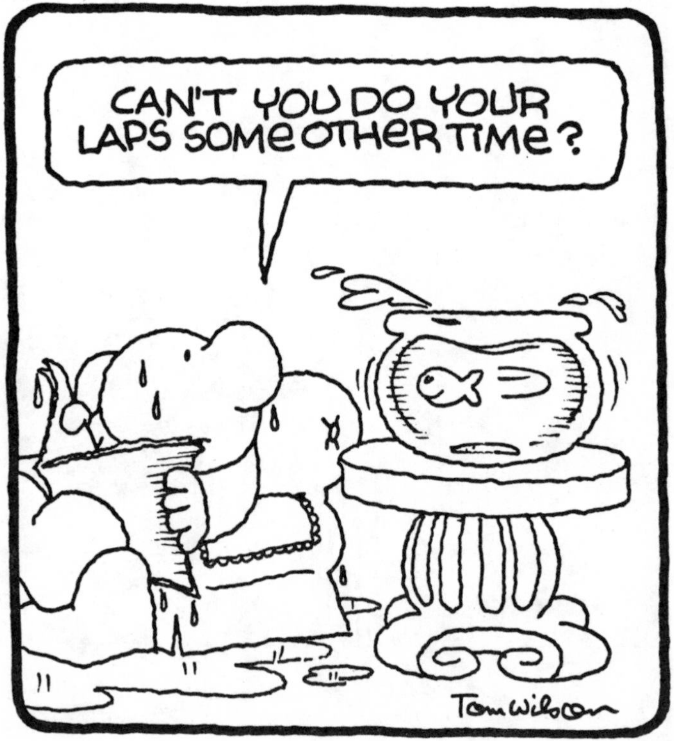
CAN'T YOU DO YOUR LAPS SOME OTHER TIME?
Tom Wilson

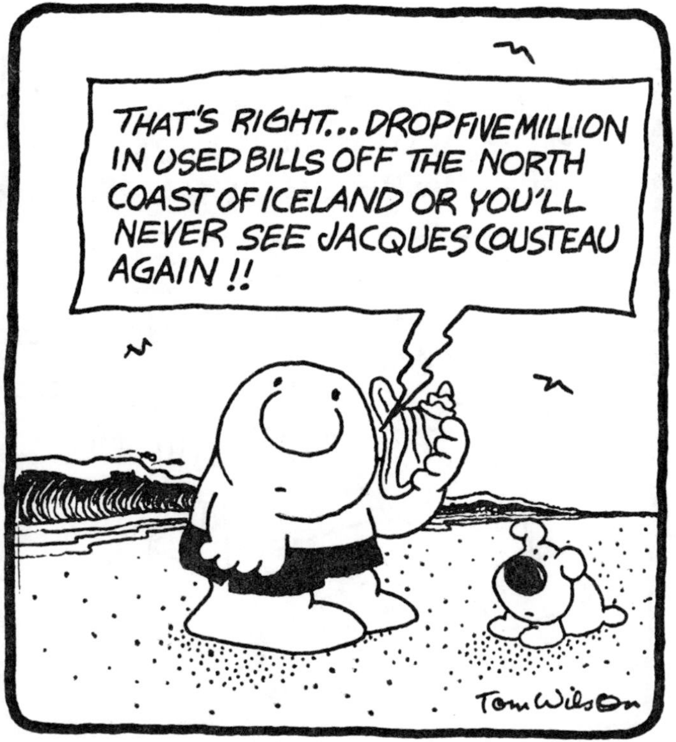
THAT'S RIGHT... DROP FIVE MILLION IN USED BILLS OFF THE NORTH COAST OF ICELAND OR YOU'LL NEVER SEE JACQUES COUSTEAU AGAIN !!
Tom Wilson

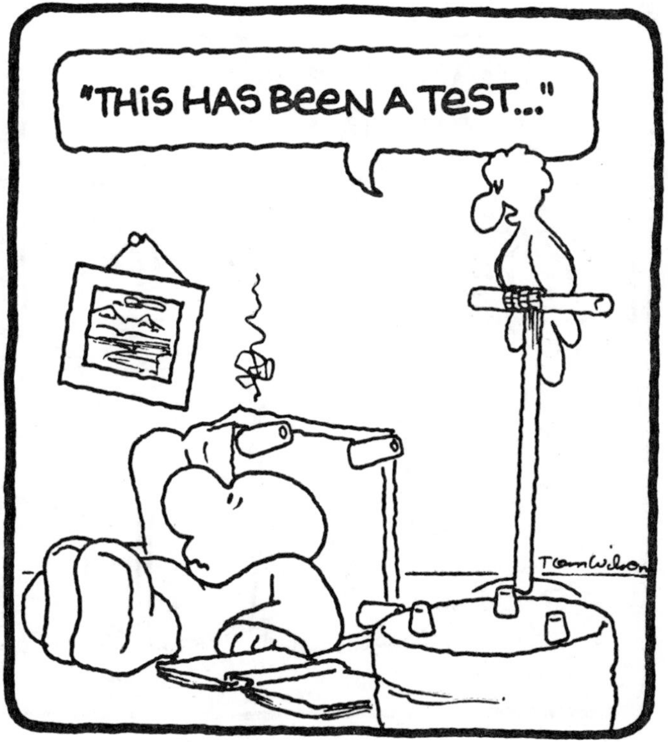
"THIS HAS BEEN A TEST..."
Tom Wilson

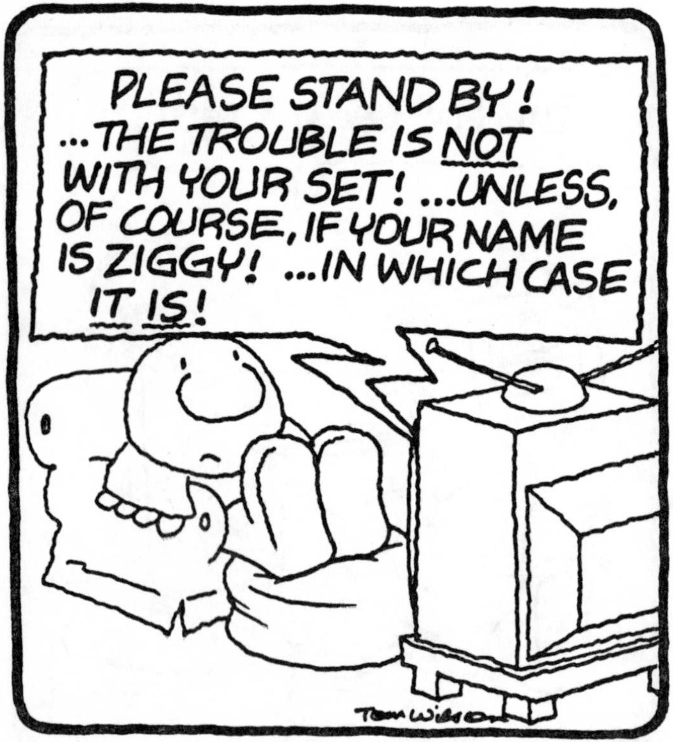
PLEASE STAND BY! ...THE TROUBLE IS NOT WITH YOUR SET! ...UNLESS, OF COURSE, IF YOUR NAME IS ZIGGY! ...IN WHICH CASE IT IS!
TOM WILSON

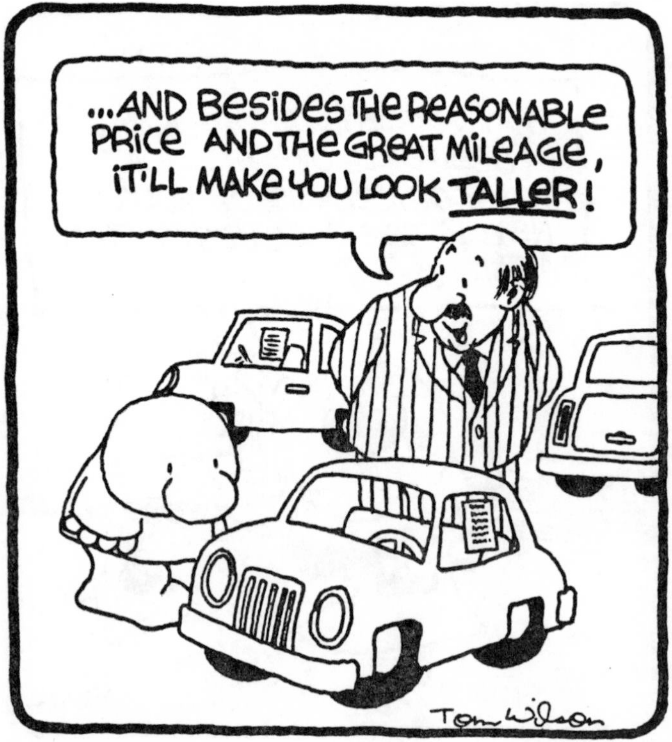
...AND BESIDES THE REASONABLE PRICE AND THE GREAT MILEAGE, IT'LL MAKE YOU LOOK TALLER!
TOM WILSON

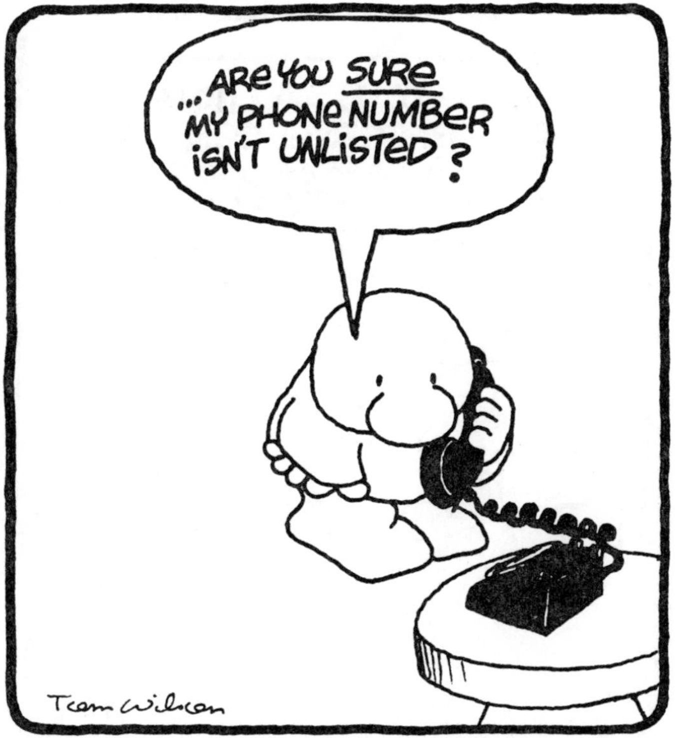
...ARE YOU SURE
...MY PHONE NUMBER
ISN'T UNLISTED ?
Tom Wilson

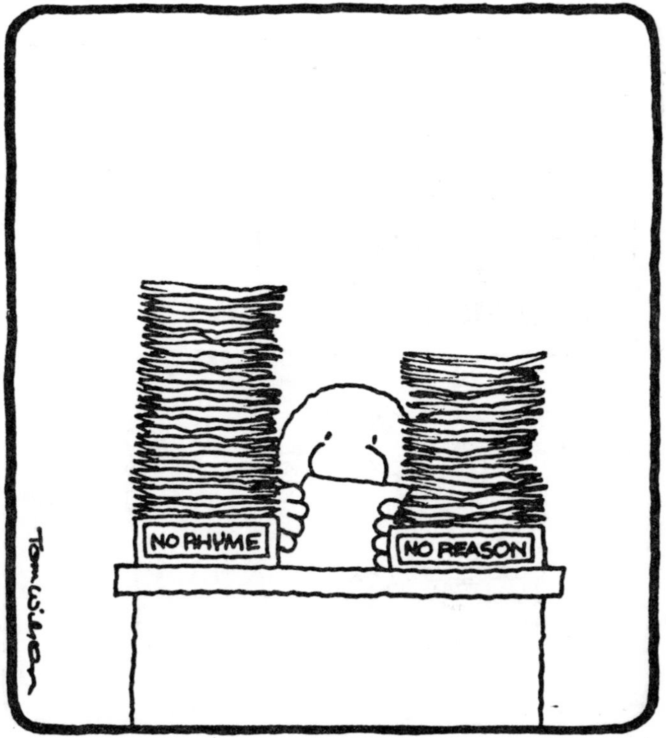
NO RHYME
NO REASON
Tom Wilson

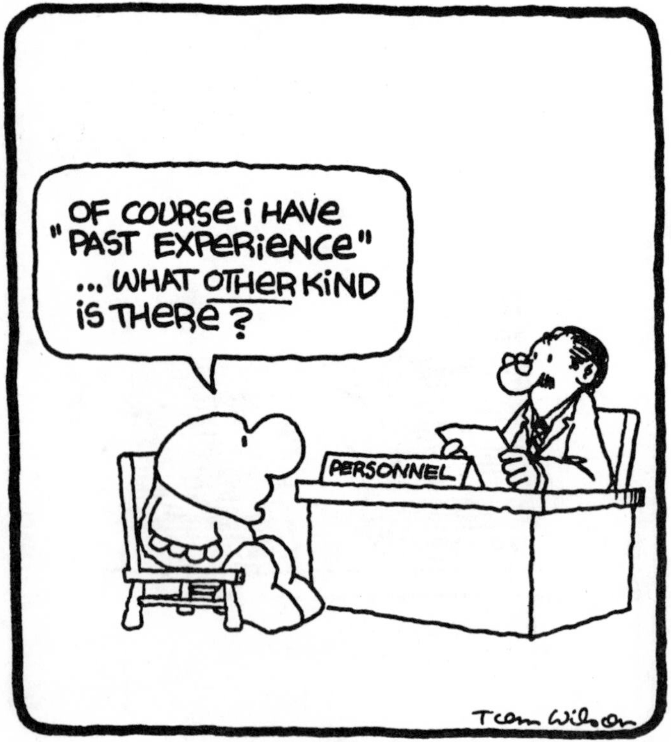
OF COURSE i HAVE "PAST EXPERiENCE" ... WHAT OTHER KiND iS THERE ?
PERSONNEL
Tom Wilson

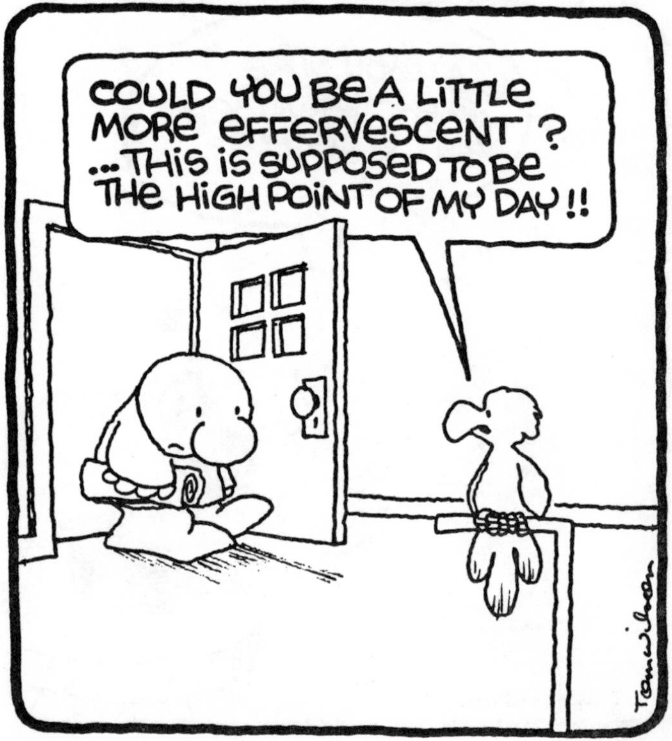
COULD YOU BE A LiTTLE MORE EFFERVESCENT ? ...THiS iS SUPPOSED TO BE THE HiGH POiNT OF MY DAY !!
Tom Wilson

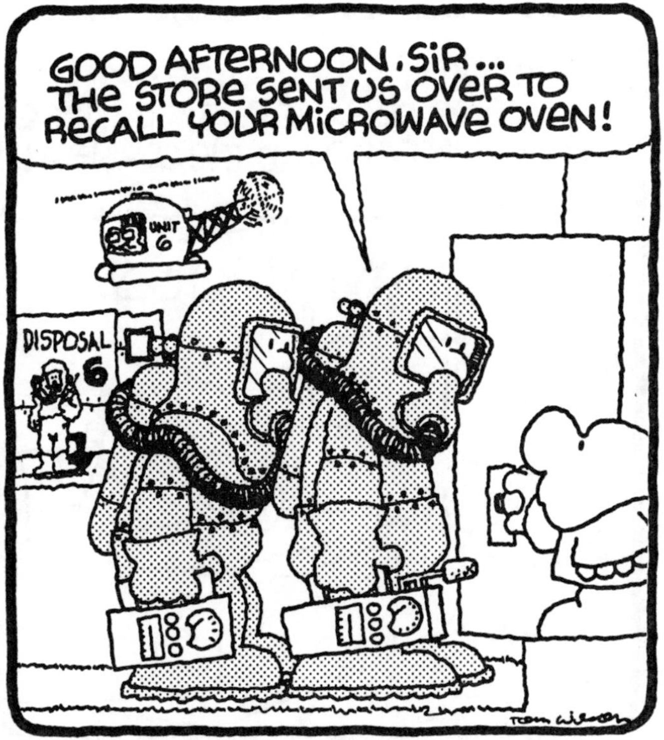
GOOD AFTERNOON, SiR... THE STORE SENT US OVER TO RECALL YOUR MiCROWAVE OVEN!
UNIT 6
DISPOSAL 6
Tom Wilson

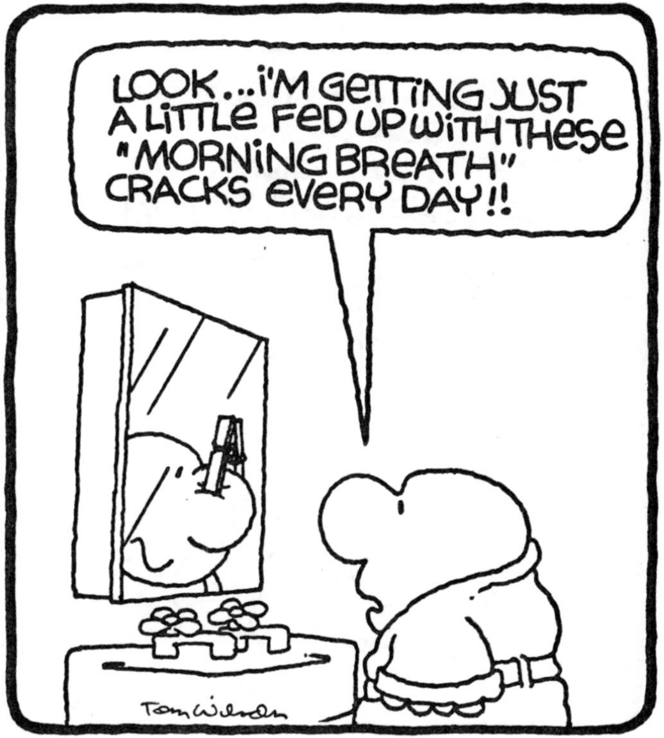
LOOK...i'M GETTiNG JUST A LiTTLE FED UP WiTH THESE "MORNiNG BREATH" CRACKS EVERY DAY!!
Tom Wilson

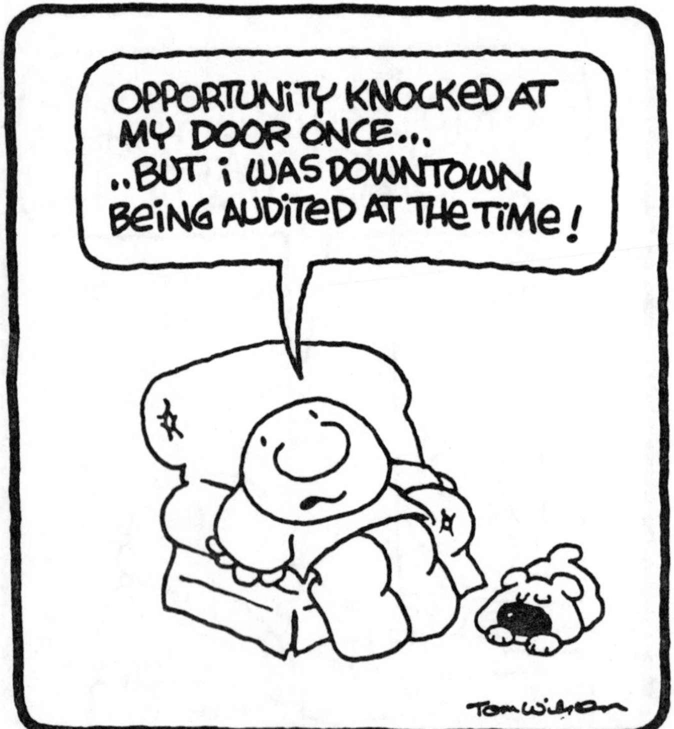
OPPORTUNITY KNOCKED AT MY DOOR ONCE... ..BUT i WAS DOWNTOWN BEING AUDITED AT THE TIME!
Tom Wilson

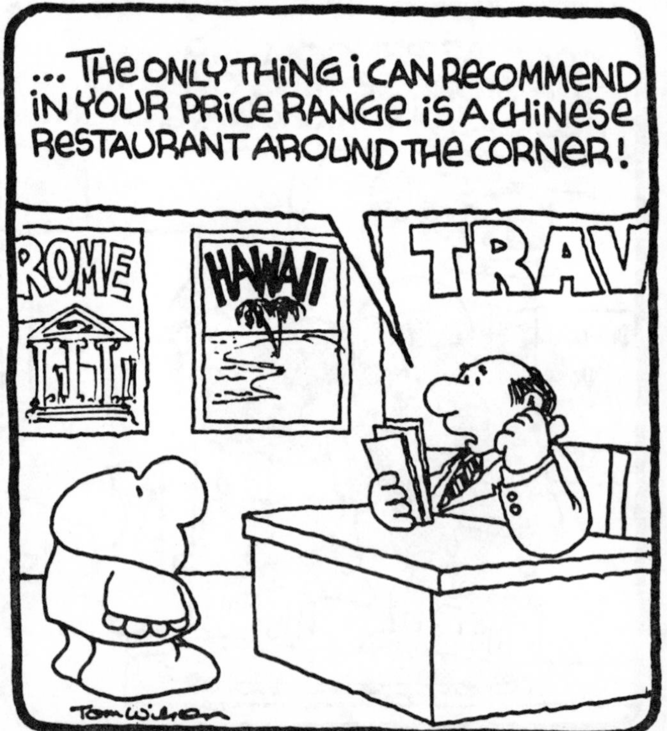
...THE ONLY THING i CAN RECOMMEND IN YOUR PRICE RANGE IS A CHINESE RESTAURANT AROUND THE CORNER!
ROME
HAWAII
TRAV
Tom Wilson

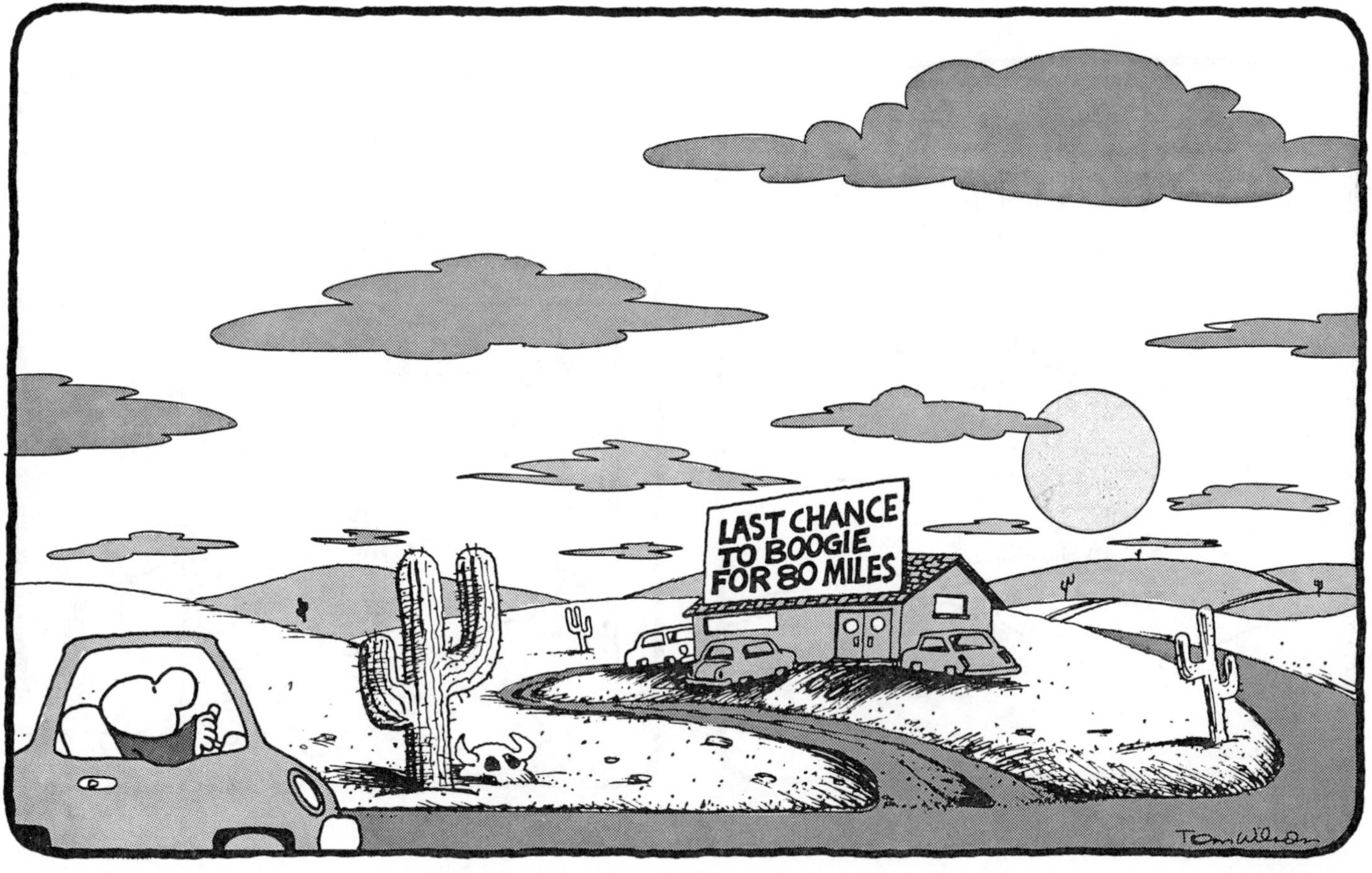
LAST CHANCE
TO BOOGIE
FOR 80 MILES
Tom Wilson

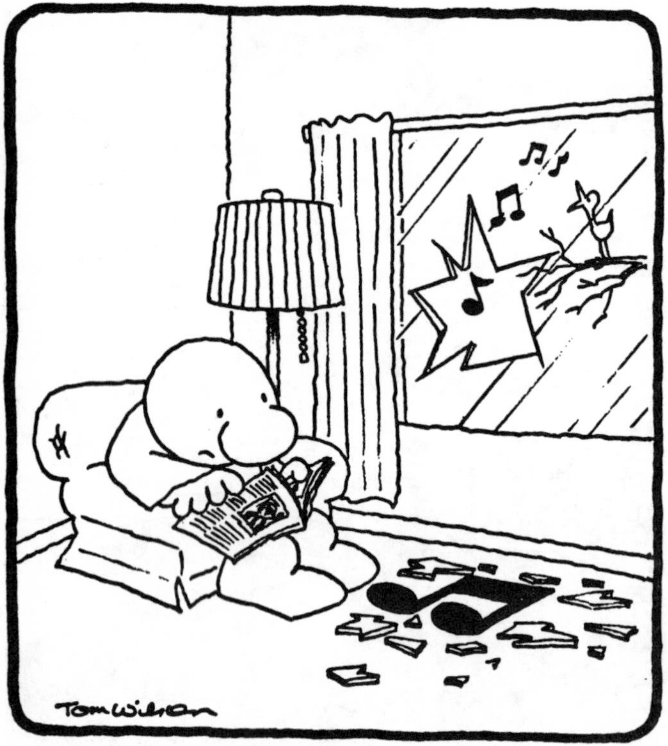

Tom Wilson

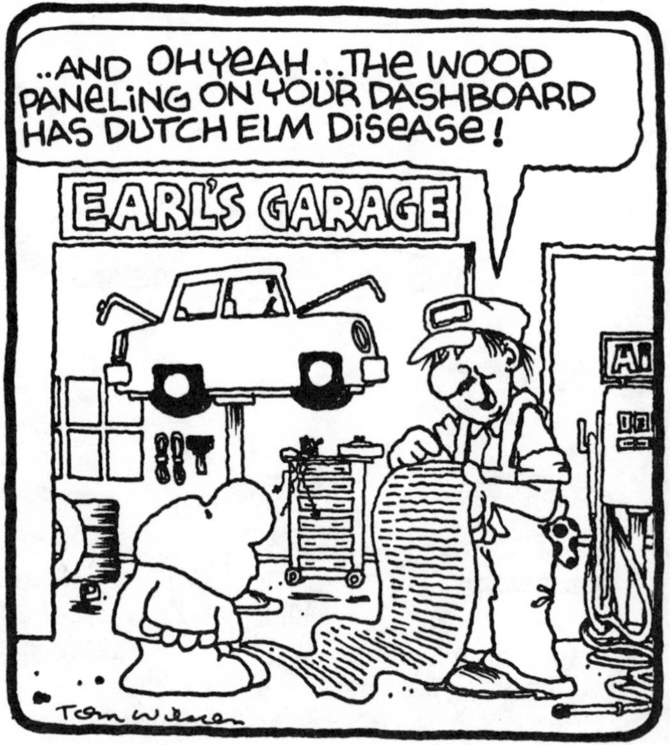

..AND OH YEAH...THE WOOD PANELING ON YOUR DASHBOARD HAS DUTCH ELM DISEASE!
EARL'S GARAGE
Tom Wilson

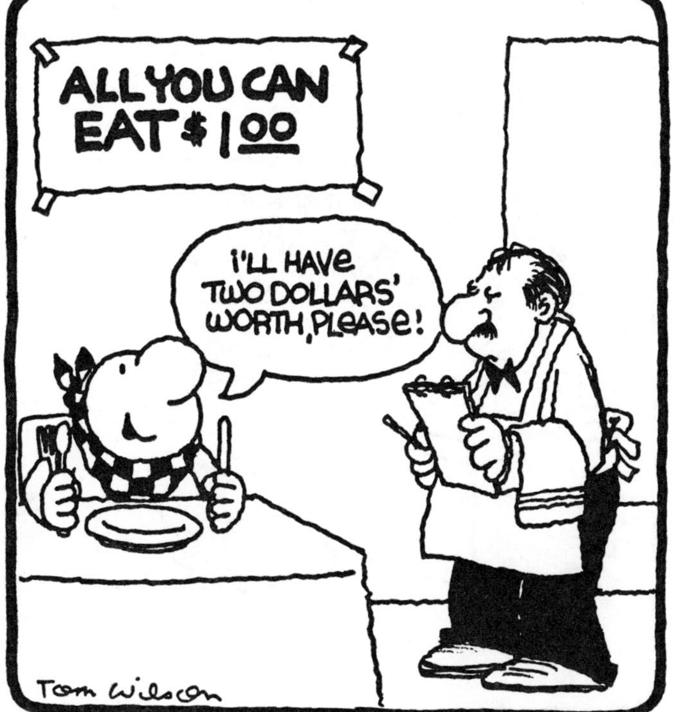
ALL YOU CAN EAT $1.00
I'LL HAVE TWO DOLLARS' WORTH, PLEASE!
Tom Wilson

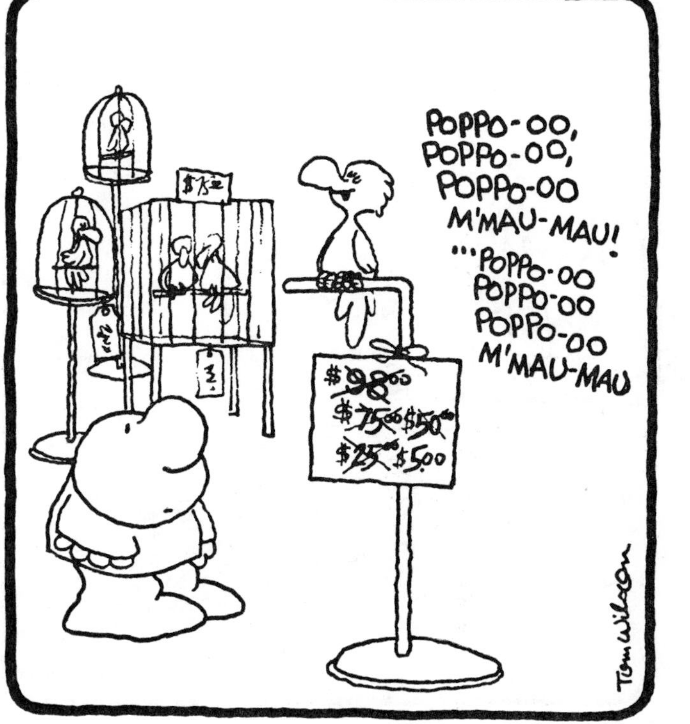
POPPO-OO, POPPO-OO, POPPO-OO M'MAU-MAU! ...POPPO-OO POPPO-OO POPPO-OO M'MAU-MAU
$98.00 $75.00 $50.00 $25.00 $5.00
Tom Wilson

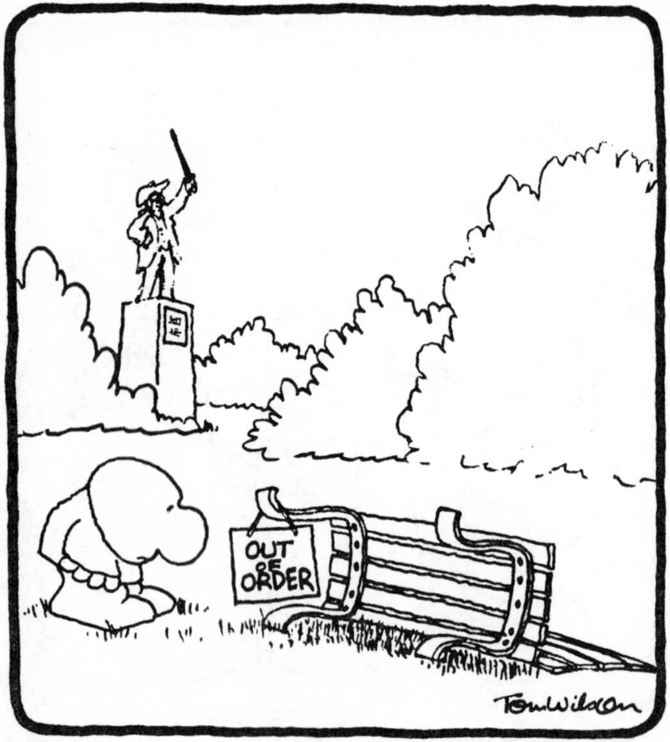
OUT OF ORDER
Tom Wilson

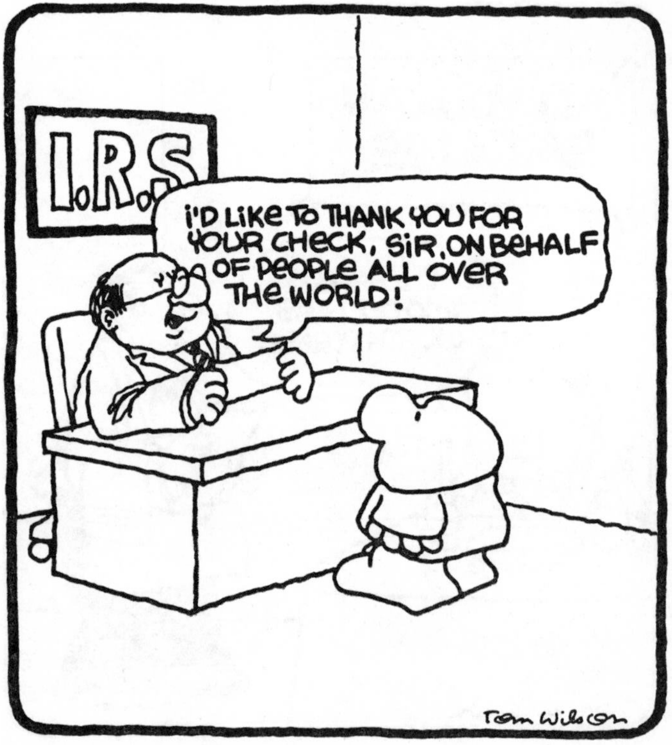
I.R.S.
I'D LIKE TO THANK YOU FOR YOUR CHECK, SIR, ON BEHALF OF PEOPLE ALL OVER THE WORLD!
Tom Wilson